THE FACTS ON
ISLAM

JOHN ANKERBERG
JOHN WELDON &
DILLON BURROUGHS

HARVEST HOUSE PUBLISHERS

EUGENE, OREGON

Cover by Dugan Design Group, Bloomington, Minnesota

Cover photos © iStockphoto

Back cover author (Dillon) photo © Goldberg Photography

THE FACTS ON ISLAM
Updated edition
Copyright © 1992/2008 by The John Ankerberg Theological Research Institute
Published by Harvest House Publishers
Eugene, Oregon 97402
www.harvesthousepublishers.com

Library of Congress Cataloging-in-Publication Data
Ankerberg, John, 1945-
The facts on Islam / John Ankerberg, John Weldon; updates by
Dillon Burroughs.
   p. cm.—(The facts on series)
ISBN-13: 978-0-7369-2218-0
ISBN-10: 0-7369-2218-0 (pbk.)
1. Islam—Controversial literature. I. Weldon, John. II. Burroughs,
Dillon. III. Title.
BT1170.A55 2008
297—dc22
                                                          2008001043

Printed in the United States of America

08 09 10 11 12 13 14 15 16 / VP-SK / 10 9 8 7 6 5 4 3 2 1

Contents

Section Four
Islam—A General Critique

Section Five
The Accuracy of the New Testament Text

Encouraging Communication and Critique

Apart from Christianity, Islam is probably the most influential religion on earth. It is the second-largest religion in the world, with between 1 and 1.5 billion followers worldwide. Islam may be the fastest-growing religion in the world; whether it eclipses Christianity is uncertain. In addition, a powerful resurgence of Islamic fundamentalism radicalism continues to spread the Muslim faith into more moderate Islamic nations.

What is the difference between the terms *Islam* and *Muslim?*

Islam is the correct name for the religion that the Muslim prophet Muhammad claimed God (Allah) revealed to him through the angel Gabriel. The name *Islam* is derived from the infinitive of the Arabic verb "to submit" (to Allah's will). *Muslim* is the correct term for a follower of Islam and comes from the present participle of the same verb.[1]

More than any other single factor, the followers of Islam have their lives directed by the book they believe is the Word of God—the Qur'an. Dr. J. Christy Wilson of Princeton University comments, "Next to the Bible, it is the most esteemed and most powerful book in the world."[2] Whatever Muslims believe and do, it is the teachings in the Qur'an that have inspired these beliefs and actions. This is why no one should underestimate its importance.

The book you hold serves two purposes. First, it

supplies a critique of Islam from the perspective of history and Christian faith. Second, it's designed to encourage those familiar with this information to seek appropriate and effective ways of communicating with their Muslim friends. The material in this book is introductory—primarily to inform Christians and non-Muslims about Islam as it relates both to Christian and Muslim truth claims.

Regrettably, Muslims often have a number of unfortunate misunderstandings concerning Christianity. Muslims may also be very sensitive to even valid criticisms about Islam, the Qur'an, or Muhammad, so dialogue can be difficult. Help on effectively relating to Muslims can be found in the resources listed at the end of this book. We emphasize that any Christian desiring to help Muslims spiritually will find it helpful to continue studies in this area.

Qur'an translations

Muslims may refuse to accept any translations of the Qur'an.* Nevertheless, a good English translation does provide sufficiently accurate meanings of the original. The translations we have chosen to cite are

- that of *A.J. Arberry*, which in the words of Wilfred Cantwell Smith of Harvard University, is "the one that comes closest to conveying the impression made on the Muslims by the original";[3]

- that of the Iranian scholar *N.J. Dawood*, director of Contemporary Translation Limited and managing director of

---

* While Muslims may be critical of non-Muslim translations, we should not necessarily conclude that Muslim translations are always more accurate. For example, "Muslim translators such as Yusuf Ali will not hesitate to mistranslate the Arabic text [compare Sura 5:76] in order to keep the English reader from discovering obvious errors in the Quran.... The readers of his translation must be aware of its hidden apologetic agenda."[4]

the Arabic Advertising and Publishing Company, Ltd., London;

- that of *J.M. Rodwell,* which "has been declared by modern scholars to be one of the best translations ever produced";[5]

- and that by *Abdullah Yusuf Ali,* called *The Holy Qur'an,* widely used among American Muslims and considered by them to be among the best of translations.

Indeed, "some Muslims are prepared to commend the accuracy of the best of these translations, and to admit their value as interpretation, though not official interpretation, of the meaning of the sacred text."[6]

Finally, it should be noted that the different traditions of Islam (such as Sunni, Shi'ite, and Sufi) have, correspondingly, quite different interpretations of the Qur'an.

The Religion of Islam:
Introduction

1

What is Islam?

Islam is the world religion founded by an Arabian visionary named Muhammad (about AD 570–632; also spelled *Muhammed* or *Mohammed*), who was born in the city of Mecca in what is now Saudi Arabia. Muhammad claimed he received supernatural revelations from God through the angel Gabriel. These revelations were written down by others and compiled into a book called the Qur'an, the Muslim Bible (also spelled Koran).

Today, Islam is comprised of two principal schools—the majority Sunni school (90 percent) and the minority Shi'ite school (10 percent). In addition, there are millions of Muslim mystics called Sufis. In America, Muslim influence is seen in traditional Islam as well as the Black Muslim movement.[1] It is commonly believed there are now as many as five to eight million Muslims in America. A number of authorities place the number more accurately at around two million; whatever the exact number, it will apparently continue to expand for the foreseeable future.[2]

2

Why is Islam important?

Islam is important for the following reasons. First, there are over one billion followers of Islam in the world. Second, the collective power of Islam is able to dramatically influence the world economy through OPEC, especially with oil at over $100 a barrel at present and expected to remain at high levels. Or, its minority radical side, through major terror attacks such as 9/11, in addition to the loss of life and the resulting worldwide war on terror, has wreaked destruction that will soon exceed a trillion dollars in direct and indirect costs. Third, the growing religious influence of Islam outside traditionally Islamic nations such as in Europe and Africa is unmistakable. Fourth, Islam has the ability to play a key role in the social stability or instability of dozens of governments around the world. Fifth, minority radical Islamism constitutes the leading anti-democratic force in the world, and a principal goal of much if not all of Islam is to bring Islamic law (Shari'a law) to every nation.[3]

Islam is vitally important because it has the power to change the destinies of hundreds of millions of people—including those in the United States. Further, Arab nationalism and the Muslim religion have become the single most crucial issue in the volatile Middle East, an ongoing focal point for the attention of the entire world. No one can know how a major crisis in that region may ultimately affect the rest of the globe. But the possibilities are sobering.[4]

The influence of Islam in the modern world is increasing daily in other ways. As noted, it is the first or second fastest-growing religion in the world, and in that role it now dominates more than 40 countries on three continents. It is the driving force behind numerous nations in the Middle East, Africa, and Asia. Indeed, over 30 countries now have populations that are at least 87 percent Muslim. It has also become the second-largest religion in Europe and the third or fourth largest in the United States. Islam is now the second largest religion in Britain also. In 1974, France had one mosque—today there are more than 1,700. There are now more Muslims than Methodists in Chicago, over 150 Muslim Student Organizations on U.S. college campuses, and over 2,000 mosques or similar places of worship in the United States.[5]

Finally, the ideological influence of Islam expands to other nations on an ongoing basis, and Islamic fundamentalism is increasingly aggressive. Muslim radicals (that is, those who are sympathetic to or wish to see Shari'a law ruling their nations) are estimated at 10 to 15 percent, or 100 to 150 million Muslims globally. Religiously, socially, politically, economically, and militarily, Islam will continue to powerfully impact our world. Nor should Christian readers of this book think Islam is of little concern to the church. The 2007 World Watch Persecution Index, published by Open Doors, revealed that six of the top ten worst countries in terms of persecution of Christians were Muslim nations, a statistic that more or less seems to hold true every year. We will discover some of the reasons for this unfortunate situation as we continue.

3

How did Islam begin?

Islam began with the supernatural visions and revelations Muhammad claimed he received from God through the angel Gabriel beginning in AD 610. Because Muhammad was illiterate and could neither read nor write, these revelations were first memorized and then later written down by his followers. The authoritative

Cambridge History of Islam discusses these revelations by noting,

> Either in the course of the visions or shortly afterwards, Muhammad began to receive "messages" or "revelations" from God...He believed that he could easily distinguish between his own thinking and these revelations...Muhammad continued to receive the messages at intervals until his death.[6]

In addition to these revelations, the personality of Muhammad played an important role in the success of Islam. His character was both complex and contradictory. In *The World's Religions*, J.N.D. Anderson, an authority on both comparative religion and Islamic law, describes the leader's temperament:

> The adult Muhammad soon showed signs of a markedly religious disposition. He would retire to caves for seclusion and meditation; he frequently practiced fasting; and he was prone to [revelatory] dreams...He was generous, resolute, genial, and astute: a shrewd judge and a born leader of men. He could, however, be cruel and vindictive to his enemies: he could stoop to assassination; and he was undeniably sensual.[7]

One of the leading biographers of our modern era, Robert Payne, observes that "violence and gentleness were at war within him."[8]

In conclusion, Islam began as a consequence of visions received by Muhammad. Whatever Islam has accomplished historically, whatever it is today, it results largely from these visions received by Muhammad some 1,400 years ago.

However, at the end of his life, Muhammad failed to name a successor. This failure resulted in the major division of Islam—into the majority Sunni and minority Shi'ite branches, each claiming to be true Islam. These divisions disagree as to the legitimate successor of Muhammad and over who offers the most accurate representation of Islamic faith.[9]

Who rightly succeeded Muhammad?

Sunnis believe that the leader of Islam does not need to be related to Muhammad. Shi'ites believe the leader must be a direct descendent. Therefore, after Muhammad's death, Sunnis followed Abu Bakr (a rich merchant among the first converts to Islam and the first Muslim caliph) and Umar (the second caliph), and Uthman (the third Muslim caliph, who burned all variations of the Qur'an) as successors of Muhammad. Shi'ites believe Ali was the true successor of Muhammad.

4

What are the basic Muslim beliefs?

Every Muslim must hold to six basic beliefs, or articles, of Islamic faith. They are as follows:

Faith in Allah. Muslims believe there is only one true God and that his name is Allah. His will is supreme.

Angels. Muslims believe in angels—such as Gabriel (called Jabril), who allegedly transmitted to Muhammad different portions of the text later collected together to form the Qur'an.

The holy books. Muslims believe that Allah has given a long series of revelations, including the Old and New Testaments, or at least parts of them. But these revelations end with the Qur'an, which supersedes all others.

For all practical purposes, Muslims accept only the Qur'an as the Word of God. For example, they believe Allah's earlier revelations in the Bible have been corrupted or are falsely interpreted by Jesus and Christians, so the authority of the Qur'an is needed for proper understanding.*

The prophets. Muslims believe Allah has sent 124,000 prophets to mankind, although only about 25 are mentioned in the Qur'an. Six of the principal prophets are Adam, the chosen of Allah; Noah, the preacher of Allah; Abraham, the friend of Allah; Moses, the speaker of Allah; Jesus, the word of Allah; and Muhammad, the apostle of Allah.

Because Muhammad's revelation is considered the greatest of all, he is called the "Seal of the Prophets" and "Peace of the World," in addition to more than 200 other appellations.

Predestination. In a form of fatalism, Muslims believe everything that happens, both good and evil, is predestined by Allah's will, his unchangeable decree.

The Day of Judgment. Muslims believe that on this day the good and evil deeds of men will be placed on a "scale." Muslims who have sufficient personal merit and righteousness (and the favor of Allah) will go to eternal heaven; all others will go to eternal hell.

These required articles of faith are also related to specific Muslim practices.

---

* Because Muslims rely on this idea so heavily in their interaction with Christians, we have provided documentation showing why the New Testament documents are accurate and truthful. If they choose to deal fairly with the historical evidence, Muslims must logically accept the reliability of the New Testament text (see question 18).

5

What religious duties are required of all Muslims?

Every Muslim must practice at least five fundamental religious duties. These are known as the Pillars of Islam. They are considered required observances, upon which the Muslim faith rests. These are so central to the practice of Islam that if you do not do these, then as many good works as you do, they cannot earn you heaven. All of these must be done.

The first pillar is reciting the creed of Islam—"There is no God but Allah and Muhammad is his prophet."

The second pillar involves prayer. The Muslim must recite prescribed prayers five times each day. Each time he must adopt a set of physical postures such as standing, kneeling, and then hands and face to the ground. The call to prayer is sounded by a Muslim *muezzin* (crier) from a tower called a *minaret*. This is part of the Muslim church or public place of worship called the *mosque*.

The third pillar is the religious duty to observe the month of fasting called *Ramadan*. This fast commemorates the first revelation of the Qur'an that Mohammad received in the year 610. Although eating is permitted at night, for an entire month Muslims must fast during daylight hours.

The fourth pillar of Islamic duty is to give alms to the poor. Muslims are required to give 2.5 percent of their earnings plus other forms of wealth, as determined by a complicated system.

The fifth and last pillar is that of the *hajj*, a pilgrimage to Mecca, Muhammad's place of birth. This is required at least once during the lifetime of every Muslim who is physically and financially able to make the trip (unless he is a slave).

No space available?

Dr. Emir Caner, a former Muslim who converted to Christianity and now serves as a seminary dean, shared the following in an interview with us: "Here is a great problem for Muslims. More than two million Muslims a year go to Mecca now, and it's absolutely overpopulated and cannot handle any more. The average Muslim lives about 70 years or less. If you assume that there is no duplication, that every year the hajj is formed of two million new people, then only 140 million Muslims can ever visit Mecca in that time span. Yet there are 1.4 billion Muslims now. Now if only 10 percent can go, what hope is there of heaven for the other 1.2 billion Muslims on planet Earth?"[10]

A sixth religious duty is often associated with the above five pillars, although it is considered optional by some. This is obedience to the call of *jihad*. Jihad may be interpreted as internal (spiritual struggle) or external ("defending" Islam) or both. Though the term has evolved over the ages and modern Muslim apologists often assert its softer side, throughout most of history and today, jihad primarily connotes that warfare has spiritual significance.

For example, when the situation warrants it, this duty requires Muslims to go to war to defend Islam against its perceived enemies. Thus, al-Qaeda and related groups believe that in waging a war of terror against Israel, America, and the West, they are "defending" Islam because the Western worldview is seen as hostile to Islam (theologically, politically, and culturally), threatening both its preservation and expansion.

Anyone who dies in a holy war is considered a martyr for Islam and is allegedly guaranteed eternal life in heaven; unfortunately, something that has become a powerful motivation for today's suicide bombers. Moreover, such martyrdom is considered heroic among many devout Muslims.

In the early 1990s, the Iraqi dictator Saddam Hussein attempted to gather support for his takeover of Kuwait and his war against American forces by issuing a call to Muslims for a holy war against the West. Although this largely failed because of Hussein's blatant secularism, it did not fail entirely. The end result was over 100 terrorist actions committed against America and Western interests in the first month of the war, not to mention massive demonstrations against the West in many Islamic countries.

Similarly, the horrific acts of 9/11 were the result of a jihad against the West declared by Osama bin Laden and other extremist Islamic leaders. Those who volunteered to fight were encouraged in part by the Qur'an's promises that terrorist martyrs would be guaranteed eternal life in heaven.

Prayer is needed

Besides Christian missions, the most powerful agent against radical Islam is the bravery of many moderate Muslims, former Muslims, Christians, and secularists who are currently making great sacrifices to counter its influence. Those such as Irshad Manji, Ayaan Hirsiali, Steve Emerson, Daniel Pipes, and Walad Shoebat deserve the prayers and support of us all.

The Theology of Islam: Is It Compatible with Christian Belief?

6

What does Islam teach about Allah? Is Allah just another name for the God of the Bible?

Islam teaches that the true God is the Muslim deity, Allah. All other views of God are false because the Qur'an teaches, "The true religion with God is Islam." The Qur'an categorically states of Allah, "There is no God but he, the Living, the everlasting."[1]

But who is Allah? Is he the same as, similar to, or absolutely different from the God of Christian faith? As we will see, the Muslim God is entirely different from the biblical God.

His nature

First, the Qur'an stresses that Allah is one person only:

> They are unbelievers who say, "God is the Third of Three" [an error-filled representation of the one Triune God of Christianity]. No god is there but one God. If they refrain not from what they say, there shall afflict those of them that disbelieve a painful chastisement.[2]

The Qur'an wrongly teaches that the Christian Trinity is three gods—the Father, Mother (Mary), and Son (Jesus). For example, Sura 5:116 says, "And behold! God will say: O Jesus the son of Mary didst say unto men, 'Worship me and my mother as gods' in derogation of Allah."

Here, the Qur'an emphasizes that Christians are unbelievers because they accept the doctrine of the Trinity. But the Bible unmistakably tells us that God has revealed himself as triune, as one God eternally existing in three Persons—Father, Son, and Holy Spirit (see Matthew 28:19; John 1:1,14; Acts 5:3-4).[3] Although many Muslims believe otherwise, Christians do not believe in *three* gods, but in *one* God in whose nature reside three Persons. The Islamic idea is a clear misrepresentation of Christian belief. Christians are not polytheists who accept three gods, but monotheists who believe in one God.

His character

Second, the Muslim God has a different character than the biblical God. It is significant that of the "99 beautiful names for Allah," which Muslims memorize and use for worship, not one is "love" or "loving." The Qur'an stresses that Allah loves only those who do good, and that he does not love those who are bad. Allah himself emphasizes he does *not* love the sinner.[4] Rather, he loves those who are worthy. Thus, the love of Allah is not the love of the God of the Bible. The biblical God does love the sinner. In fact, he loves all sinners, though he does not love the sin:

> Christ died for the *ungodly*…God demonstrates his own *love* for us in this: while we were *still sinners*, Christ died for us…If when we were God's *enemies*, we were reconciled to him through the death of his Son, how much more, having been reconciled, shall we be saved through his life? (Romans 5:6,8,10).

Essentially, Allah is a God of power, not a God of love. But the Bible declares, "God *is* love" (1 John 4:6).

Further, through predestination of all things, Allah is considered the direct author of *both* good and evil. This is not the same God as described in the Bible. While the biblical God is sovereign and permits evil, he is not its direct cause. Even when it is part of his plan, he frequently turns it to a higher good, as seen in the death of Jesus for our sins, Joseph being sold into slavery (Genesis 45:8; 50:20), and in Romans 8:28: "We know that in all things God works for the good of those who love him, who have been called according to his purpose." Again, the biblical God is not the direct author of evil. Rather, he is infinitely holy and righteous (1 Samuel 2:2; Psalms 77:13; 99:9; Revelation 15:4), and his "eyes are too pure to look on evil" (Habakkuk 1:13).

His comprehensibility

Third, Allah is ultimately unknowable and incomprehensible. In *Who Is Allah in Islam*, Abd-al-Masih writes, "Allah is the unique, unexplorable, and inexplicable one—the remote, vast, and unknown God. Everything we think about him is incomplete, if not wrong. Allah cannot be comprehended."[5]

In "What Is Allah Like?" Georges Houssney writes,

> We humans can never know Allah, because he is so far from us and so different from us. The only knowledge Muslims may admit to is knowledge about Allah, not a personal, experiential knowledge of him. People cannot know Allah and should not even try to know him. Allah is not involved in the affairs of humans.

Thus, Houssney goes on to point out the contrast between Muslim and Christian concepts concerning humanity's relationship to God: "The Christian claim that humans can have a relationship with God is considered by

Muslims to be a metaphysical impossibility."[6] Whereas the Christian knows God lives inside them and they can talk to him anytime and expect he will respond, such a personal relationship is unthinkable for a Muslim.

Not who, but what

"To Muslims, Allah has not revealed himself, but rather he has revealed his *mashi'at* (desires and wishes, that is, his will)," writes Georges Houssney. "His will, according to Islamic teaching, is limited to Islamic law. A person performs the will of Allah when he follows the dictates of the Islamic legal system."[7]

Houssney further illustrates the divide between Muslim and Christian concepts of God:

> Allah has no personality and is indescribable by any characteristic attributable to man. Most of his attributes are absolute qualities which are unique to himself, like adjectives of majesty. Although some of his attributes may appear to be relational, such as mercy, they are nonmutual and one-directional. According to the Islamic doctrine of Allah, he is nonrelational. To claim that Allah is relational is to make him dependent on his creation.[8]

Two opposing concepts

All this stands in contrast to the biblical teaching that men and women *can* know God personally on an intimate, relational level. Consider these verses:

- Jesus said, "This is eternal life, that they may *know* You, the only true God, *and Jesus Christ* whom You have sent" (John 17:3 NASB).

- Jesus, speaking of the Holy Spirit: "You know him, for he lives with you and will be in you" (John 14:17).

- Jesus, speaking again: "On that day you will realize that…you are in me" (John 14:20).

- "Jesus replied, 'If anyone loves me, he will obey my teaching. My Father will love him, and we will come to him and make our home with him'" (John 14:23).

- The apostle Paul prayed for Christian believers concerning God, "that you may *know* him better" (Ephesians 1:17).

- The apostle John emphasized, "We *know* that we have come to *know* him if we obey his commands. The man who says, 'I know him,' but does not do what he commands is a liar, and the truth is not in him" (1 John 2:3-4).

- Thus, John emphasized, "Dear friends, let us love one another, for love comes from God. Everyone who loves has been born of God and *knows* God. Whoever does not love does not *know* God, because God is love" (1 John 4:7-8).

The above reveals that the Muslim God, Allah, and the biblical God, Yahweh, constitute two distinct and opposing concepts of God. Because Muslims teach that Allah alone is the one true God, they claim that Christians worship a false god. Yet, if Allah is the true God, Muslims know they will never have a personal relationship with him.

7

What does Islam teach about Jesus Christ?

Muslims claim they believe in the true Jesus Christ. They praise Jesus as a prophet of God, as sinless, as "the

Messiah," as "illustrious in this world and the next,"[9] as "the Word of Allah," and as "the Spirit of God." Muslims cite the Qur'an in confirmation of their belief in Jesus: "And we gave Jesus, Son of Mary, the clear signs, and confirmed Him with the Holy Spirit."[10]

Unfortunately, however, Islam does not believe in the *biblical* Jesus. The Bible teaches that Jesus is God's one and only Son. Jesus himself taught this:

> God so loved the world that he gave his *one and only Son,* that whoever believes in him shall not perish but have eternal life…Whoever believes in him is not condemned, but whoever does not believe stands condemned already because he has not believed in the name of *God's one and only Son* (John 3:16,18; see also Matthew 11:27; 26:64).

God himself declared of Jesus at his baptism, "This is my Son, whom I love; with him I am well pleased" (Matthew 3:17; 17:5). Further, the apostles Paul and John also declared that Jesus is God's Son (Romans 1:3; 1 John 5:9-12). In fact, virtually every book in the New Testament either declares or assumes that Jesus is God's unique Son.

Neither the Son of God nor deity of any kind

On the other hand, Islam asserts that Jesus was merely one of God's many prophets or messengers, and not God's only Son; in fact, that he was superseded by Muhammed. Muslims thus strongly reject the idea that Jesus is the Son of God.[11] The Qur'an repeatedly emphasizes that Jesus Christ is *not* the literal Son of God:[12]

- "It is not for God to take a son unto Him."

- "They say, 'God has taken to Him a son'…Say:

'Those who forge against God falsehood shall not prosper.'"

- "Praise belongs to God, who has not taken to Him a son."

- "Warn those who say, 'God has taken to Himself a son';…a monstrous word it is, issuing out of their mouths; they say nothing but a lie."

- "They are unbelievers who say, 'God is the Messiah, Mary's Son.'"

Muslims hear Christians as somehow implying God had physical relations with someone and had a son. But this is not what Jesus claimed or what Christianity teaches. Rather, through the virigin birth, God the Son took on human form and became the God-man, Jesus Christ.

In summary, the Qur'an emphatically denies that Jesus Christ is the Son of God—a teaching Jesus himself just as emphatically affirmed (John 3:16,18; 10:36-38). The Christian view of Jesus Christ as God's literal Son is considered blasphemous to Muslims.[13] Christians agree that Jesus was not the product of a sexual union, but disagree that the miraculous birth resulted in a mere prophet.

How could Muslims believe it, however? Even the Qur'an teaches Jesus was miraculously virgin-born. Sura 3:47 reads that Mary "said, 'O my Lord! How shall I have a son when no man hath touched me?' He said, 'Even so, Allah creates what he wills.'" The end result in Islam is that Jesus is a prophet—but not the Son of God as Jesus himself taught. Ali's translation of Sura 5:73,78 reads, "They do blaspheme who say: 'God is Christ the son of Mary.'…Christ the son of Mary was no more than an apostle."[14]

Obviously, then, Muslims deny that Jesus Christ was God incarnate, or God in human form. Any Muslim who believes that Jesus Christ is God has committed "the one unforgivable sin," called *shirk* (here, equating Jesus with God, that is, Allah)—a sin that will send him to hell forever.[15] The Qur'an clearly teaches that Jesus was only a man: "The Messiah, Jesus Son of Mary, was only the Messenger of God." Sura 43:59 asserts, "Jesus was no more than a mortal whom [Allah] favored and made an example to the Israelites."[16]

The Qur'an has Jesus deny his own deity

When Allah asks Jesus if he is God, Jesus replies, "It is not mine to say what I have no right to."[17] In fact, even as a baby, according to Sura 19:20,34, Jesus praised his birth and then said, "I am the servant of Allah."

A prophet who was not crucified

Further, Muslims do not believe Jesus was crucified and died on the cross. They believe Allah would never permit this to happen to one of his special prophets. When Muslims deny that Christ was crucified on the cross and teach instead that God substituted someone else in his place, they reject the clearest teaching of the New Testament. Even Jesus prophesied—repeatedly— that he had to go to the cross and that this was God's direct will for him:

> From that time on Jesus began to explain to his disciples that he must go to Jerusalem and suffer many things at the hands of the elders, chief priests and teachers of the law and that he must be killed and on the third day be raised to life (Matthew 16:21).
>
> Jesus took the Twelve aside and told them, "We are going

up to Jerusalem, and everything that is written by the prophets about the Son of Man will be fulfilled. He will be handed over to the Gentiles. They will mock him, insult him, spit on him, flog him and kill him. On the third day he will rise again" (Luke 18:31-33).

Islam has a problem at this point. It can be shown historically that Jesus predicted his own imminent and violent death on about a dozen separate occasions. However, the Qur'an says Jesus is a great prophet. But if Jesus said he would die a violent death on the cross and didn't, then that would make him a false prophet. The Qur'an would be wrong that Jesus was a true prophet and would thus be discredited. On the other hand, if Jesus did die as he predicted, then he is indeed a great prophet. But this would contradict the Qur'an, which says he didn't die on the cross. Either way, the Qur'an is discredited.

Finally, Islam teaches that Muhammad was a superior prophet to Jesus because he brought God's final and best revelations to man. Badru D. Kateregga, head of Islamic studies and comparative religion at the University of Nairobi, Kenya, exemplifies the Muslim view of Jesus as an inferior prophet to Muhammad:

> The truth that all the previous prophets have proclaimed to humanity was perfected by Prophet Muhammad… The Qur'an, which is Allah's *final guidance* to mankind, was revealed to the Prophet Muhammad…the seal of all prophets, 600 years after the Prophet Isa (Jesus)… Muhammad…is the *one prophet* who fulfilled Allah's mission during his lifetime.

> Muslims believe in and respect all the prophets of God who preceded Muhammad…They *all* brought a uniform message—Islam—from Allah. Muhammad is the last in

seal of prophethood. Through him, Islam was completed
and perfected. As he brought the last and latest guidance
for all mankind, it is *he alone* to whom Muslims turn for
guidance.[18]

Thus "Muhammad…is the last prophet and messenger
of Allah. His mission was for the whole world and
for all times" (Sura 4:35). In other words, Muslims
must not turn to Jesus for spiritual guidance, only to
Muhammad.

A prophet, a fraud, or a savior?

Quite a few of the issues we have raised about Jesus
are brought to life by former Muslims Ergun and Emir
Caner in the following story, which they related during
an interview:[19]

> **Ergun**: We walked into the mosque and we would study
> about Jesus—Isa, we called Him. When I walked into
> the church, I thought it would be the same Isa. And so
> the pastor asked me, "Well, what do you think about
> Jesus?" I said, "Oh, we respect Him. He's a prophet."
> Long line of prophets. We even have an entire chapter
> of the Qur'an—Sura 19, "Maryam," named after His
> mother, Mary.
>
> The Qur'an is very clear as to who Jesus is in Islam: that
> He was born of a virgin—they have no problem with
> that. That He is the Word—they have no problem with
> Jesus as *halima* because He is communication. They even
> have no problem with the term *messiah*, because it means
> "the Anointed One," and He was anointed for that task.
> But the Qur'an is very clear: "Say not trinity…desist from
> it." "Hath Allah begotten a son?" Sura 19:88, is one of
> the ones I have open on my lap right here.
>
> The pastor then said, "You can't do this."

And I said, "What do you mean?"

He said, "Well, you don't believe Jesus was crucified?"

"No. We do not."

He said, "All right, forget the crucifixion for a minute. Why was He indicted?"

"Well, He was indicted for two reasons: for sedition among the Romans, and for blasphemy by the Jews."

The pastor said, "What was the blasphemy? It was that Jesus claimed to be God."

And the pastor said, "So let's just forget for a second that He was crucified. If Jesus claimed to be God, could that Jesus be a prophet in Islam?"

I said, "No. He would be a fraud. He would be a liar. Because you are not allowed to claim any pretense to being God."

And the preacher said, "So if Jesus said He was God, you cannot simply respect Him. You must either revere Him as the One He actually said He was, or reject Him as a fraud. But He simply could not be in the line of prophets." Now, this hit me between the eyes.

Emir: Then it was a year later after my brother was saved that I was invited to a revival. The thing that struck me most was, first, as Muslims, we understood Allah loves those who do righteous deeds. And all of a sudden we hear that "while we were yet sinners Christ died for us" [Romans 5:8]. And it hit me right between the eyes. Christ became what He always was—personal. He loved us intimately and unconditionally and wanted to have a relationship with us. And it wasn't about "scales" of judgment, it was about a Savior.

And that really did what was necessary—that is, to introduce the true Jesus to us.

John Ankerberg: Emir, what was it like when it first dawned on you that, in Islam, you had not been told the truth about Jesus? What was that transition like?

Emir: Well, when you have to look at that, you also have to say, "Where does the origin of the false prophecy come from but Muhammad?" So my people say, "You can't speak harshly about a prophet where one of five people on earth believe him and revere him as a prophet." But that's exactly what we had to do. We had to come to an end of the "excellent example," that is, Muhammed, as chapter 33 of the Qur'an says. Instead, Muhammad is not our "excellent example" or exemplar, he is someone who cannot be trusted, because he had false prophecy—that is, false revelation: a false message, a false hope, and a false god. We came to an end of our religion.

Far greater than any prophet

As we have already seen, Muslims communicate an inaccurate picture. Jesus Christ is far more than one of God's messengers or prophets. He is God's one and only Son (John 3:16-18). Further, he is the second Person of the Trinity, God incarnate—God himself (John 1:1,14; 5:18). Jesus claimed to be both Lord and God: "You call me 'Teacher' and 'Lord,' and rightly so, for that is what I am" (John 13:13). "Anyone who has seen me has seen the Father [God]" (John 14:9). "I and the Father [God] are one" (John 10:30).

In conclusion, both the Qur'an and Islam are in error concerning their teachings about the most important man of history, Jesus Christ. Islam claims that it honors and reveres Jesus, but it rejects what the Bible teaches about him and what he taught about himself. Further, no history scholar outside Islam goes to the Qur'an to find out information about Jesus. The Qur'an, at best, is fifth-hand testimony—coming to us, it is said, through the angel Gabriel to Muhammad, then to different scribes who wrote down what Muhammad said, whose surviving writings were then collected by Uthman and put into the Qur'an—all 600 years after Christ lived. The New Testament, in contrast, is eyewitness testimony by Matthew, Mark (via the apostle Peter), Luke (via the apostle Paul), and John, all written within 20 to 60 years after Jesus lived.*

Jesus' undeniable assertion

Keep in mind the clear answer Jesus gave the Jewish Sanhedrin when he was on trial for his life. He was asked the question, "Are you the Christ [Messiah], the Son of the Blessed One [the Son of God, that is, deity]?"

"I am," said Jesus, "and you will see the Son of Man sitting at the right hand of the Mighty One and coming on the clouds of heaven" (Mark 14:61-62).

8

What does Islam teach about salvation?

Because the Qur'an teaches that "the true religion with God is Islam," this means for the Muslim that salvation is achieved only through obedience to the teachings of Allah. Salvation in Islam requires that a person must be a member of the Islamic faith. "Whoso desires another religion than Islam, it shall not be

---

* There is also testimony from pagan sources—Roman history from the first century recorded by Tacitus, which confirms the death of Jesus on a cross under Pontius Pilate. In all, five non-Christian sources in existence support the fact that Jesus died on a cross: Tacitus, Lucian, Mara bar Serapion, and two others.

accepted of him; in the next world he shall be among the losers." As a result, "those who disbelieve, and die disbelieving—upon them shall rest the curse of God and the angels, and of men altogether, there indwelling forever; the chastisement shall not be lightened for them; no respite shall be given them."[20] For Islam, there is only one way to God. All others are wrong.

But what exactly does the Muslim believe about salvation? Here are five basic points that reveal what the religion of Islam teaches about salvation.

A. Islam teaches that forgiveness is conditioned upon good works and Allah's choice of mercy

Islam is a religion of salvation by personal effort. In other words, the Muslim thinks that by striving to please God and doing good works, he or she will hopefully gain entrance to heaven through personal accomplishments.

The Qur'an clearly teaches that salvation is achieved on the basis of good works. Consider the following statements:[21]

> ...Every soul shall be paid in full what it has earned.

> ...God loves those who cleanse themselves.

> Gardens of Eden, underneath which rivers flow, there indwelling forever; that is the recompense of the self-purified.

Islam teaches that on the Day of Judgment a person's good and evil deeds will be weighed on a scale. Good works must outweigh the evil deeds. The person whose balances are heavy with good deeds will go to heaven, while the person whose scales are light will go to hell. The Qur'an asserts that on the Day of Judgment they whose balances shall be heavy with good works, shall be happy; but they whose balances shall be light, are those who shall lose their souls, and shall remain in hell forever.[22]

With knowledge We will recount to them what they have done, for We are watching over all their actions. On that day, their deeds shall be weighed with justice. Those whose scales are heavy shall triumph, but those whose scales are light shall lose their souls, because they have denied Our revelations.[23]

Salvation in Islam is centered upon the works done by each individual. The list of good works necessary to enter heaven is long and includes that he or she 1) accept only the Muslim God Allah and his prophet Muhammad, 2) do good works and all that is required of him or her by Allah (the Pillars of Islam), and 3) be predestined to heaven by Allah's favor.

The uncertainty of salvation in Islam. Given such requirements, it is not surprising that almost no Muslims have assurance of salvation. In the book *Sharing Your Faith with a Muslim,* Abdiyah Akbar Abdul-Haqq comments that the Islamic reliance on good works is bound to leave any Muslim who seeks personal assurance of salvation "utterly confused"[24]—because in this life no Muslim can ever know if his good works are finally sufficient—let alone if he is predestined to Allah's favor.

William Miller, a missionary to Muslims in Iran from 1919 to 1962, discusses the Islamic view of salvation—its dependence upon good works and personal merit, and the uncertainty which this brings to the heart of every Muslim:

Islam has no Savior. Mohammad is rarely called Savior. He is said to have brought God's laws to men, and they, by keeping those laws, must satisfy God's requirements and win His approval…Since many Muslims realize that they [fall short of Qur'anic standards]…they recite extra prayers in addition to those required for each day, they make gifts to charity, and go on pilgrimages not only to Mecca, but also to other sacred shrines, in order to gain merit, and if possible, balance their account with God. But since God does not make known how the accounts of His stand, a Muslim facing death does not know whether he is to go to paradise or to hell. After all, the decision is made by the arbitrary will of God, and no one can predict what that decision will be…And so the Muslim lives and dies, not sure of his final salvation.[25]

Forgiveness in Islam. The Muslim concept of forgiveness is unlike that of biblical Christianity. In biblical Christianity, forgiveness is based upon the death of Christ on the cross as a *past* action. Christ is not only the one who provides salvation, he *became* our salvation. This means that once a person receives Christ as his or her Savior, all of his or her sins are forgiven and they are *guaranteed* a place in heaven: "I tell you the truth, whoever hears my word and believes him who sent me *has eternal life and will not be condemned*" (John 5:24) and further,

> Praise be to the God and Father of our Lord Jesus Christ! In his great mercy he has given us new birth into a living hope through the resurrection of Jesus Christ from the dead, and into an inheritance that can *never perish, spoil or fade—kept in heaven for you,* who through faith are shielded by God's power until the coming of the salvation that is ready to be revealed in the last time (1 Peter 1:3-5).

In Islam, it's just the opposite. There is no atonement for sin—no propitiatory basis for forgiveness of sins. Each Muslim must pay for his own salvation by doing good deeds. Moreover, Allah simply forgives those whom he chooses to forgive and he forgives only those who have done enough good deeds to outweigh their bad deeds. Again, this forgiveness is conditioned upon *both* personal merit and Allah's choice of mercy. Muslims never know if their personal works are enough that their sins will be forgiven or if Allah will, in the end, be merciful to them. Muslims certainly hope they will be saved. But the following statements in the Qur'an, as well as others, indicate the conditional nature of forgiveness in Islam:

> And whosoever of you turns from his religion, and dies disbelieving—their works have failed in this world and the next; those are the inhabitants of the Fire; therein they shall dwell forever.[26]

> God has pardoned what is past; but whoever offends again, God will take vengeance on him; God is Almighty, Vengeful.[27]

Only one had to pay

The Bible teaches of Jesus, "He is the atoning sacrifice for our sins." Because of his great love for us, Jesus willingly died in our place (John 10:18), taking the penalty due our sin so that God could freely forgive us. "God presented him [Jesus] as a sacrifice of atonement" and "God did it to demonstrate his justice at the present time, so as to be just and the one who justifies those who have faith in Jesus" (Romans 3:25-26).

Can certainty be found? For a Muslim, if 51 percent of his deeds are good ones, the other 49 percent are simply forgiven. Allah just wipes the slate clean. But this is contrary to what the Bible teaches—a person's full salvation comes completely by God's grace through faith

of whom it says, "He forgave us *all* our
s 2:13). God does not allow any sins to
he can't. He is totally just and honest.
ty for every sin, which is an offense to
God. Therefore, Jesus paid for all our sins. The Bible
also emphasizes that salvation does not depend in part
on good works nor come by them or by anything else we
can do to please God with our own efforts: "We maintain that a man is justified by faith apart from observing
the law" (Romans 3:28). "It is by grace you have been
saved, through faith—and this *not from yourselves*, it is
the gift of God—*not by works*, so that no one can boast"
(Ephesians 2:8-9).

In contrast to the teachings of Islam, the Bible
teaches that anyone who wishes may confidently *come*
to God, *freely* receive salvation, and *know* for certain he
or she is eternally saved at the very moment of salvation. Jesus taught, "God so loved the world that he gave
his one and only Son, that whosoever believes in him
shall *not* perish but *have* eternal life" (John 3:16). The
apostle Peter taught, "The Lord…is patient with you,
not wanting anyone to perish, but *everyone* to come to
repentance" (2 Peter 3:9).

Again, Jesus taught, "He who believes [at that
moment] *has* eternal life" (John 6:47) and "I am the
Alpha and the Omega, the Beginning and the End.
To him who is thirsty I will give to drink *without cost*
from the spring of the water of life" (Revelation 21:6).
The apostle John emphasized, "I write these things
to you who believe in the name of the Son of God so
that you may *know that you have eternal life*" (1 John
5:13). "Since we have been justified through faith, we
have peace with God through our Lord Jesus Christ"
(Romans 5:1).

B. Islam teaches that Jesus Christ was neither crucified nor resurrected; therefore, salvation cannot possibly be had through faith in Christ

We mentioned earlier that Islam rejects the atoning sacrifice of Christ on the cross. One reason for this is its view that people are basically good. If people are not unredeemed sinners, they do not need a Savior from sin. Instead, the focus is on good works, preserving one's life by abstaining from evil, and gaining Allah's favor. Also, as we saw in the previous question, because Islam considers Jesus Christ one of Allah's prophets, it is unthinkable to Muslims that God would permit one of his prophets to be crucified. Therefore, Islam denies that Christ died upon the cross. The Qur'an teaches,

> They denied the truth and uttered a monstrous false-hood...They declared: "We have put to death the Messiah, Jesus the son of Mary, the apostle of Allah." They did not kill him, nor did they crucify him, but they thought they did.[28]

Because Muslims do not believe that Christ died on the cross, they are forced to also deny his resurrection. A leading public defender of Islam, Ahmad Dedat, claims,

> Throughout the length and breadth of the 27 books of the New Testament, there is not a single statement made by Jesus Christ that "I was dead, and I have come back from the dead." The Christian has been belaboring the word resurrection. Again and again, by repetition, it is conveyed that it is proving a fact...[But] Jesus Christ never uttered the word that "I have come back from the dead," in the 27 books of the New Testament, not once.[29]

But Mr. Dedat is wrong. On many occasions in the

New Testament, Jesus predicted both his death *and* his resurrection. For example, he told his disciples, "The Son of Man must suffer many things and be rejected by the elders, chief priests and teachers of the law, and he must be killed *and on the third day be raised to life*" (Luke 9:22). After his resurrection he declared to his disciples,

> This was what I told you while I was still with you: Everything must be fulfilled that is written about me in the Law of Moses, the Prophets and the Psalms...He told them, "This is what is written: The Christ will suffer and rise from the dead on the third day, and repentance and forgiveness of sins will be preached in his name to all nations" (Luke 24:44,46,47).

Further, in Revelation 1:18, Jesus taught, "I am the Living One; *I was dead, and behold I am alive for ever and ever!*" Again, if Islam teaches that Jesus is an honored prophet, then Jesus could not have lied when he said he would rise from the dead. (And to reiterate, Muslims cannot claim a corrupted text to prove their teachings, as we demonstrate in question 18.)

No return

Muslims say Jesus Christ will not come back at the end of time. There will be no second coming. But in Matthew 16:27, Matthew 25:31, and elsewhere, Jesus also predicted his literal, physical return to earth to set up his kingdom.

Atonement is unneeded in Islam. Dr. John Elder, a missionary to Muslims in Iran from 1922 to 1964, discusses the Muslim rejection of the atonement and the reasons upon which it is based:

Like the doctrine of the death of Jesus, the ordinary Muslim completely rejects the doctrine of Jesus' atonement for sin. He rejects it first on historical grounds. If Jesus survived the cross [that is, never truly died], as the Muslim believes, then He could not have given His life to atone for man's sins.

In the second place, the Muslim idea of God and His decrees recognizes no need for atonement. According to the doctrine of decrees, God determined the fate of all men from the beginning, and we are helpless to change it. This belief is taught in many places in the Qur'an…

A third reason why Muslims deny the possibility of an atonement is their belief that God does not love man, and indeed, is unaffected by man's actions…Any idea that God so loved the world that He gave His only son is completely foreign to the Muslim mind…. Thus, a pious Muslim is constantly performing acts which he explains by saying, "savab darad" (it is meritorious). Thus, he saves for most of his lifetime to make the Meccan pilgrimage; he gives money to help erect a mosque; he faithfully reads the Qur'an even though it be in a language he does not understand; and he prays the prescribed Arabic prayers.[30]

In sum, Muslims reject the biblical teaching that Christ died for their sins and, instead, seek salvation by religious observance.

C. The concept of the loving God of the Bible is difficult for the Muslim to accept

In Islam, Allah's "love" is not based on his unconditional commitment and self-sacrifice, as is biblical love, for example, "God *demonstrates* His own love toward us, in that while we were yet sinners, Christ died for us"

(Romans 5:8). In Islam, Allah's love is conditional—based on our prior performance and Allah's mysterious divine decree. In Islamic theology, much like Buddhist philosophy, the concept of love is primarily that of "mercy," in that Allah grants a prescribed way to work your way into being accepted by him. It is very impersonal, rather than personal.

Dr. J. Christy Wilson of Princeton University observes that the concept of God's love is foreign to Islamic thinking also because of the extreme emphasis placed upon Allah's sovereign power and transcendence:

> Most Muslims will misunderstand and question the statement of the New Testament that "God is love." His power and sovereign transcendence over all creation are so emphasized in Islam that to call Him a God of love or to address Him as "Father" would be far from Muslim thought.[31]

John Elder further comments, "In addition to the idea that God does not need men and therefore cannot love, the Muslim commonly cites two main problems in believing that God is love: the existence of sin and pain, and man's insignificance in the vastness of the universe."[32] Here, ironically, Islam uses many arguments about the problem of evil that atheists do.

In stark contrast, the Bible declares that "God *is* love" (1 John 4:16).*

D. Muslim salvation is fatalistic

We have discussed the fact that the Muslim concept of forgiveness is conditioned upon good works. On the one hand, we find in the Qur'an the promise of

---

* For answering atheistic arguments about a loving God and the problem of evil, see our articles on this topic at johnankerberg.org.

heaven for those who do good. But on the other hand, the promise is conditional—one must possess the true religion of Islam, obey its precepts, and—very importantly—find favor with Allah. At this point, Islam's salvation appears to become fatalistic.

The issue of predestination. The largest apparent conflict in the Muslim concept of salvation is Allah's predestination. The Qur'an teaches, "All things have we created after a fixed decree." Further, "God leads astray whomsoever He will; and He guides whomsoever He will."[33] Abdul-Haqq observes, "There are several [Muslim] traditions also about the predestination of all things, including all good and bad actions and guided and misguided people...Even if a person desires to choose God's guidance, he cannot do so without the prior choice of God in favor of his free choice. This is sheer determinism."[34]

Dr. Wilson comments, "The fifth article of [Muslim] faith is predestination...the fact that everything that happens, either good or bad, is foreordained by the unchangeable decrees of Allah. It will be seen at once that this makes Allah the author of evil, a doctrine that most Muslim theologians hold." The Qur'an teaches, as Wilson points out, "And if a good thing visits them, they say, 'This is from God'; but if an evil thing visits them, they say, 'This is from thee.' Say: 'Everything is from God.'"[35] And,

> The man whom Allah guides is rightly guided, but he who is led astray by Allah shall surely be lost. As for those that deny Our revelations, *We have predestined for hell many jinn and many men*...We will lead them step by step to ruin...

> None can guide the people whom Allah leads astray. He
> leaves them blundering about in their wickedness...Say:
> "I have not the power to acquire benefits or to avert evil
> from myself, except by the will of Allah."[36]

Islamic fatalism is why we often hear Muslims using the
phrase "If God wills."

Death in battle. At first glance there does appear to be
one way a Muslim can guarantee his salvation. This is
found in connection with the Muslim concept of *jihad*,
or holy war. Achieving security of salvation requires
death in battle: "If you are slain or die in God's way...it
is unto God you shall be mustered."[37] And,

> When you meet the unbelievers in the battlefields strike
> off their heads and, when you have laid them low, bind
> your captives firmly...Thus shall you do...As for those
> who are slain in the cause of Allah...he will admit them
> to the Paradise he has made known to them.[38]

It appears at first that Muslims are promised heaven
for death in battle. But even this security of salvation is
conditioned on something else—bravery:

> O believers, when you encounter the unbelievers
> marching to battle, turn not your backs to them. Whoso
> turns his back that day to them, unless withdrawing
> to fight again or removing to join another host, he is
> laden with the burden of God's anger, and his refuge is
> Gehenna—an evil homecoming![39]

Even in the "guarantee" of heaven through death in
a holy war, the Muslim promise of salvation appears to
remain provisional. (But no Muslim strapping on a suicide belt is told this.) Biblically speaking, unnumbered
Muslims trusting in Islam to save them and take them

to heaven have instead been sent to an eternity without Christ in the jihads of history and today.

Fight your enemies

"Allah has given those that fight with their goods and their persons a higher rank than those who stay at home...The unbelievers are your sworn enemies...Seek out your enemies relentlessly...You shall not plead for traitors...Allah does not love the treacherous or the sinful."[40]

E. Do Christians have salvation according to Islam?

Some have claimed that, according to Islam, Christians can remain Christians and still inherit salvation. They also claim that the God of Islam and the God of the Bible are the same God. But this is simply false. To the contrary, the Qur'an teaches that only if Christians convert to Islam and remain good Muslims will they have the opportunity for salvation. If Christians reject the Qur'an, they are classified as unbelievers and their destiny is an eternal hell:

> God guides not the people of the unbelievers...They are unbelievers who say, "God is the Messiah, Mary's Son."... The Messiah [Jesus] said, "Children of Israel, serve God [meaning Allah], my Lord and your Lord. Verily, whoso associates with God anything, God shall prohibit him entrance to Paradise, and his refuge shall be the Fire; and wrongdoers shall have no helpers." They are unbelievers who say, "God is the Third of Three." No god is there but One God. If they refrain not from what they say, there shall afflict those of them that disbelieve a painful chastisement.[41]

In the above citation, we see that 1) Christians who believe that Jesus is the divine Messiah are classified as unbelievers; 2) even though Christians believe

God is one in nature but three in Person, according to Islam, those who believe in the Trinity (that "God is the Third of Three") are unbelievers; and 3) Christians who believe that Christ is God (those who "associate" God with Jesus—that is, commit the unforgivable sin of *shirk*) will be sent to hell. The only conclusion is that if Christians do not turn from their errors and accept Islam, they are subject to the strictest judgment:

> [In war] kill those who join other gods with God [this phrase in other translations reads, "kill those who are idolaters, pagans"] wherever ye shall find them; and seize them, besiege them, and lay wait for them with every kind of ambush: but if they shall convert, and observe prayer, and pay the obligatory alms, then let them go their way, for God is Gracious, Merciful.[42]

> Do they not know that whosoever opposes God and His Messenger—for him awaits the fire of Gehenna, therein to dwell forever?[43]

> Verily, God will not forgive the union of other gods with Himself!…And He who uniteth gods with God hath devised a great wickedness…The flame of Hell is their sufficing *punishment!* Those who disbelieve our signs we will in the end cast into the fire: so oft as their skins shall be well burnt, we will change them for fresh skins, that they may taste the torment.[44]

In sum, those who argue that Christians can be saved as Christians or that Allah and the God of the Bible are the same deity are simply mistaken.

The Bible of Islam: Is the Qur'an the Word of God?

9

What does Islam claim about the Qur'an?

As mentioned, Islam claims that the Qur'an is the literal Word of God, dictated supernaturally to Muhammad from the angel Gabriel. Muslims believe the Qur'an is perfect and without error. Musa Qutub, PhD, and M. Vazir Ali, both Muslim scholars, assert that the Qur'an is the only book ever to "withstand the microscopic and telescopic scrutiny of one and all, without the book stumbling anywhere."[1]

Islam further claims that the teachings of the Qur'an are in harmony with the words of the Bible that Christians supposedly once had. Why do Muslims believe that? Because this is what the Qur'an teaches. (Again, Islam also believes Christians have corrupted the Bible so that the Bibles Christians now use are unreliable.)

> And We have sent down to thee the Book [the Qur'an] with the truth, confirming the Book [the Bible] that was before it, and assuring it.[2]

> This Qur'an could not have been forged apart from God; but it is a *confirmation* of what is before it.[3]

As the *Encyclopedia Britannica* observes, "For the Muslims, the Qur'an is the Word of God, confirming and consummating earlier revealed books and thereby replacing them."[4]

A corrupted Bible?

Some good questions to ask Muslims are, If Allah gave Christians the uncorrupted Bible, but it then became corrupted, how could Allah have allowed this to happen to his very own word? Whatever the response, the point is this: How then can Muslims know that the Qur'an, also given by Allah, has not been corrupted as well? Further, why have the manuscript copies of the books found in the Bible been the same all the way back to the earliest copies, only a generation removed from Jesus and his apostles? And why is this not true for the Qur'an?

10

Does the Qur'an deny the Bible?

Everyone who carefully and impartially reads both the Bible and the Qur'an must agree that, as they both stand, the two books contradict one another on every major religious doctrine, including the nature of God, Jesus, salvation, and the Bible. If the New Testament was *not* corrupted, as we will soon discuss, then how could Allah be the inspiration behind the Bible *and* behind the Qur'an, which contradicts it? This would lead us to believe that God's revelations are contradictory—and therefore useless. Consider the following chart, illustrating some conditions that we documented in section II:

	The Qur'an	**The Bible**
God	unitarian	Trinitarian
Jesus	a man	God incarnate
Salvation	by works; uncertain	by grace; assured
Holy Book	corrupted historically	uncorrupted

Again, if the manuscript evidence forces us to conclude

that the Bible has not been corrupted, there is only one conclusion a Muslim can logically reach. If Allah really inspired *both* the Bible and the Qur'an, then he contradicts himself to such an extent that it is impossible to ascertain his teachings or will for humanity.

Muslims respond by saying they have been told that the Bible has indeed been corrupted and, therefore, its present teachings are untrustworthy. Only the Qur'an is pure and uncorrupted. But this argument is indefensible on historic, textual, and even Qur'anic grounds, as we will see.

In the next eight questions we will seek to determine whether the Qur'an is pure and uncorrupted as Muslims claim, and whether their claim that the Bible is corrupted and untrustworthy is really valid. Because of the eternal implications, it is difficult to overestimate the importance of this topic.

11

Does the Qur'an contain historical errors and biblical distortions?

Muslims and Christians agree that it is impossible for God to inspire error in his Word. But it can be shown that the Qur'an itself contains a large number of errors. Dr. Robert Morey, who frequently debates Muslim scholars and apologists, lists more than 100. For instance, the Qur'an teaches that the Ark of Noah came to rest on the top of Mount Judi (Sura 11:44), not Mount Ararat as the Bible teaches; that Abraham's father was Azar (Sura 6:74), not Terah as the Bible teaches; that he attempted to sacrifice Ishmael (Sura 37:100-112), not Isaac as the Bible teaches; that Pharaoh's *wife* adopted

Moses (Sura 28:8-9), not his daughter as the Bible teaches; that Noah's flood occurred in Moses' day (Sura 7:136, compare, 7:59ff.), not much earlier, as the Bible teaches; and that Mary, the mother of Jesus, gave birth to Jesus under a palm tree (Sura 19:22), not in a stable as the Bible teaches.[5]

In the preface to his translation of the Qur'an, Rodwell notes the presence of "contradictory and…inaccurate statements."[6] For example, though Muhammad is nowhere found in the Bible, the Qur'an claims Muhammad himself is "described in the Torah and the Gospel" (Sura 7:157). The disciples of Christ were obviously Christians, but the Qur'an teaches that the disciples of Christ were Muslims. Six hundred years before Muhammad was born, Christ's disciples allegedly claim, "We believe; and bear thou witness that we are Muslims."[7]

For both of the foregoing assertions, there is no historical evidence besides the Qur'an and Muslim writings. Anyone can claim anything, but there is no proof to back up all these claims. It should also be noted that no historical Jesus scholar outside Islam looks to the Qur'an as a source for historical information about Jesus, the apostles, or early Christianity. They know it is actually true that the Qur'an is unreliable.

The Qur'an also teaches that Abraham was not a Jew but a Muslim: "No; Abraham in truth was not a Jew, neither a Christian; but he was a Muslim."[8] But the Jews consider Abraham a Jew. The Christians consider Abraham a Jew. Jesus himself considered Abraham a Jew. All of the world considers Abraham a Jew—except the Qur'an.

There are also some unlikely events described in the Qur'an. For example, after Allah tempts the people to sin, the judgment for their evil is stated this way:

"When they had scornfully persisted in what they had been forbidden, we changed them into detested apes."[9] According to history, the army of Abraham, the king of Ethiopia, halted its attack on Mecca due to a smallpox outbreak. But Sura 105 teaches he was defeated by birds that dropped stones of baked clay on the soldiers.

The Qur'an and the Bible. Finally, the Qur'an has many biblical distortions. Nearly every biblical episode discussed in the Qur'an has additional or contrary information supplied: "The names and events of Old Testament books and prophets are very definitely copied in the Quran. However, often the stories in the Quran are garbled and confused."[10] For example, in Sura 2:56-57,61 the Jews returned to Egypt *after* the Exodus which, biblically and historically, was never the case. In Sura 3:41 it is stated that Zechariah would be speechless for *three days*. Biblically, however, it was until John's birth—*nine months* (Luke 1:18-20). In Sura 12:11-20 the Qur'anic story of Joseph is markedly different from the biblical story of Genesis 37; the accounts are so contrary as to demand that one of them be inaccurate. In Sura 2:241, Muhammad confuses the persons of Saul and Gideon. There are also variations in Sura 12:21-32,36-55 when compared with Genesis 37–45.[11]

Whether it is the descriptions of the creation of humanity, the Fall, Moses and the burning bush, Noah and the ark, Joseph going into Egypt; or the lives of Zechariah, John the Baptist, Mary and Jesus, or other biblical characters; the Qur'an often contradicts biblical teaching.[12]

But at the very same time it is declaring contradictory historical people and events, the Qur'an also explicitly claims to "confirm the Book of Moses and the Gospel."[13]

So if textual criticism proves the Bible is historically accurate, then it is the Qur'an that must be in error.

12

Does the Qur'an contain contradictory teachings?

The Qur'an maintains that it contains no contradictions. In Sura 4:84 Allah challenges men, "Will they not ponder on the Koran? If it had not come from Allah, they could have surely found in it many contradictions."[14] Since Allah claims to not contradict himself, then everything that has purportedly "come down from him" (the Bible, or parts of it, and the Qur'an) must be in agreement.

Muslims must believe in the doctrinal unity among the books of Allah—the Bible as originally given and the Qur'an. But we have just seen that they conflict. Further, the Qur'an contains contradictions within its own pages:

- In Sura 11 the Qur'an teaches that one of Noah's sons did not enter the ark and thus "Noah's son was drowned" in the Flood. It then contradicts this statement in Sura 21, where it declares that "we saved him [Noah] and *all* his kinsfolk from the great calamity."[15] According to the Bible, all of Noah's sons are delivered (see Genesis 6–7) and their genealogies are provided.

- The Qur'an has conflicting accounts of Muhammad's original call to be a prophet: Sura 53:2-18; 81:19-24; vs. Sura 16:102; 26:192-94; vs. Sura 15:18; 2:97.

- Sura 41:9-12 teaches it took God eight days to create the world, whereas Sura 7:51; 10:3; and 11:6 teach it took God six days.[16]

In conclusion, the above are only some of the problems faced by Muslims who believe that the Qur'an is the word of God.

Islam:
A General Critique

13

How convincing are Muslim apologetics?

In his essay "How Muslims Do Apologetics," philosopher, attorney, and theologian John Warwick Montgomery discusses a characteristic problem of Muslim apologetics—that of defending Islam primarily by "discrediting" Christianity. But "such refutations are not 'apologies' or defenses at all, but are *ad hominem* arguments of an offensive nature."[1] Even if Muslim apologists *could* disprove Christianity, this would not prove the truth of Islam. Islam would still require—on its own merits—independent verification as a revelation of God. And because the evidence is lacking, it is precisely at this point that Muslim apologists fail. Muhammad was clearly inspired by some supernatural source, but how could he have been inspired by God if his inspiration rejects God's revelation in the Bible?

Making the case

The word *apologetics* is derived from the Greek *apologia*, which means "to present a defense for."

Biblical inspiration and accuracy are independently verified by prophecy, archaeology, manuscript evidence, scientific prevision, the testimony of Christ as an infallible authority, and other means.* Islam, however,

---

* We have documented this in some detail in our *Handbook of Biblical Evidences* (Harvest House, 2008).

offers no genuine evidence for its claim that the Qur'an is inspired, other than Muhammad's own claim he was inspired by Gabriel. But what if Muhammad was wrong? If the biblical God is the true God and if Muhammad were a prophet of God, he would never have denied God's revelation in the Bible.

So how do Muslims do apologetics? First, they argue that the Christian faith is a false religion. Specifically, using the arguments of liberal theologians, higher critical methods, and rationalistic skeptics of Christianity, they reject biblical authority and the deity of Christ.[2] Second, they present arguments in defense of Islam that are convincing to Muslims but are also largely subjective and prove little or nothing.[3] In essence, Muslim apologetics are not convincing because they characteristically reject the rules of logic and evidence.* The average Muslim, unknowingly and regrettably, has been misled by apologists whose primary arguments are based on subjectivism, logical fallacies, anachronisms, and unfortunate historical errors.

14

What basic problem does the Qur'an present to Muslims?

Muslims call the Qur'an the "mother of books" (Sura 43:3), and no other book, such as the Bible, can compare to it. Suras 2:23 and 10:37-38 challenge anyone

---

* Space does not permit elaboration, except to refer the reader to taped sessions of Christian–Muslim debates and more specific evaluations of Muslim apologetic methods. For illustrations we would recommend, first, our four different television series with former Muslims Ergun and Emir Caner, available at johnankerberg.org. We also recommend the seven-hour debate between Dr. Robert A. Morey and Dr. Jamal Badawi, who some Muslims claim is the best apologist for Islam in North America. In additions, we would recommend other materials published by both Muslims and Christians.[4]

to present any other book of equal beauty. Yet, as we have indicated, the Qur'an teaches that Muslims are to accept *both* the Bible and the Qur'an:

> Say: "We believe in God, and that which has been sent down on us, and sent down on Abraham and Ishmael, Isaac and Jacob, and the [Jewish] Tribes, and in that which was given to Moses and Jesus, and the Prophets, of their Lord; *we make no division between any of them.*"[5]

The Qur'an claims that *Allah* is the God who inspired the Old Testament and the New Testament: "We gave to Moses the Book and the Salvation, that haply you should be guided." Muslims are commanded, "Observe the Torah and the Gospel...what is revealed to them from Allah."[6]

Elsewhere Muslims are told,

> O believers, believe in God and His Messenger [Muhammad] and the Book He has sent down on His Messenger [the Qur'an] and the Book which He sent down before [the Bible]. Whoso disbelieves in God and His angels and His Books, and His Messengers, and the Last Day, has surely gone astray into far error...God will gather the hypocrites and the unbelievers all in Gehenna.[7]

In the above verses we see that those who *reject* God's Books (plural) and Messengers (plural) are called unbelievers![8] Muslims are forbidden by Allah to accept only part of God's revelations. But here is a dilemma. If Muslims accept what the Qur'an teaches, they must then accept what the Bible teaches—which rejects what the Qur'an teaches.

But if a Muslim truly accepts the Bible and rejects what the Qur'an teaches, he can no longer remain a Muslim and should become a Christian.[9] So how can a Muslim trust what the Qur'an teaches when it simultaneously undermines its own authority? How does a Muslim circumvent this? By claiming the Bible's teachings have been corrupted and are untrustworthy.

15

Is the Muslim claim that the Bible has been corrupted based on facts or bias?

The Qur'an and Islam maintain that the Bible has been corrupted by Christians: "People of the Book [Jews and Christians], now there has come to you Our Messenger [Muhammad], making clear to you many things you have been concealing of the Book, and defacing many things."[10]

In his book *Christian Faith and Other Faiths*, Oxford theologian Stephen Neill observes,

> It is well known that at many points the Qur'an does not agree with the Jews and Christian Scriptures. Therefore, from the Muslim point of view, it follows of necessity that these Scriptures must have been corrupted. Historical evidence makes no impression on the crushing force of the syllogism. So it is, and it can be no other way. The Muslim controversialist feels no need to study evidence in detail. The only valid picture of Jesus Christ is that which is to be found in the pages of the Qur'an.[11]

In other words, because the Qur'an is predefined as God's perfect revelation and the Bible can be seen to contradict it, the Bible must therefore be corrupted and there is no point in further research. For Muslims, historical evidence has no relevance to the issue, because it is impossible that the Qur'an could be wrong.[12]

But this is illogical reasoning. A person must first determine if the Bible *was* corrupted. If it was not, then the error must lie with the Qur'an. And if anyone takes the time to examine and evaluate them, the historical facts prove that the Bible has not been corrupted.[13] If Muslims refuse to honestly examine and accept this evidence, it cannot be the fault of Christians. Muslims are basing their beliefs on something other than the evidence that is apparent to everyone else. For the Muslim to maintain the Bible has been corrupted is an indefensible position. (See more in question 18.)

For example...

After a thorough evaluation of the textual evidence, and citing numerous scholars in confirmation, theologians Norman Geisler and William Nix conclude that a modern critical edition of the Bible says "exactly what the autographs contained—line for line, word for word, and even letter for letter."[14]

16

Is the Qur'an uncorrupted?

Historical facts prove it is the Qur'an that has been corrupted, rather than the Bible. First, the Qur'an is not written in perfect Arabic (as it claims in Suras 12:2; 13:37; 41:41,44). Rather, it contains scores of grammatical errors and non-Arabic words.[15] Second, the text of the Qur'an itself has been corrupted. This is important since Islam claims the Qur'an is an exact word-for-word copy of God's final revelation—that is, the words inscribed on tablets that have always existed in heaven. Sura 85:21-22 says, "Nay, this is a glorious Qur'an, inscribed in a tablet preserved." But the Qur'an on earth shows something far from perfect:

There are many conflicting readings on the text of the Quran as Arthur Jeffrey has demonstrated in his book *Material for the History of the Text of the Quran*. At one point, Jeffrey gives 90 pages of variant readings on the text. For example, in Sura 2 there are over 140 conflicting and variant readings...All Western and Muslim scholars admit the presence of variant readings in the text of the Quran. Guillaume points out that the Quran at first "had a large number of variants, not always trifling in significance."...

The work of Western scholars such as Arthur Jeffrey and others has been hampered by Muslim reluctance to let Western scholars see old manuscripts of the Quran which are based on pre-Uthman texts...According to Professor Guillaume in his book *Islam* (pp. 191ff.), some of the original verses of the Quran were lost. For example, one Sura originally had 200 verses in the days of Ayesha. But by the time Uthman standardized the text of the Quran, it had only 73 verses! A total of 127 verses had been lost, and they have never been recovered. The Shiite Muslims claim that Uthman left out 25 percent of the original verses in the Quran for political reasons.

That there are verses which got left out of Uthman's version of the Quran is universally recognized. John Burton's book *The Collection of the Quran*, which was published by Cambridge University, documents how such verses were lost. Burton states concerning the Muslim claim that the Quran is perfect: "The Muslim accounts of the history of the Quran texts are a mass of confusion, contradictions and inconsistencies."

Verses which are contradictory to Muslim faith and practice have been removed from the text, such as the "satanic verses" in which Muhammad approved of the worship of the three goddesses, the daughters of Allah...

Not only have parts of the Quran been lost, but entire verses and chapters have been added to it. For example, Ubai had several suras in his manuscript of the Quran which Uthman omitted from his standardized text. Thus there were Qurans in circulation before Uthman's text which had additional revelations from Muhammad that Uthman did not find or approve of, and thus he failed to place them in his text...Western scholars have shown beyond reasonable doubt that Uthman's text did not contain all of the Quran. Neither was what it did contain correct in all of its wording...

The true history of the collection and the creation of the text of the Quran reveals that the Muslim claims are indeed fictitious and not in accord with the facts.[16]

The destruction of much of the original text

According to the previous information, even the *earliest* copies of the Qur'an must have contradicted one another or had other problems. Why? Because these copies "led to such serious disputes between the faithful" that it was necessary "to establish a text which should be the sole standard."[17] Dr. William Miller reveals that "for some years after the death of Muhammad there was *great confusion* as to what material of all that had been preserved should be included in the Koran. Finally, in the caliphate of Uthman (644–656 AD) one text was given official approval, and all [other] material was destroyed."[18]

Clearly, the earlier versions of the Qur'an must have differed significantly from this official version, as indicated in what follows:

The recording of the prophet's words in the beginning was haphazard. Verses were written on palm leaves, stones, the shoulder-blades of animals—in short, on any material which was available...Before an authorized version was established under the caliph Uthman *there were four rival editions in use.* These have long since disappeared, but we are told that they differed from the authorized version...[19]

On account of the variations and confusions which had arisen among the reported sayings of Mohammed...a revision [was] made, and all existing copies of the previous compilation [were] destroyed. Thus, the present text of the Koran is not the first edition, but a second edition.[20]

All the foregoing raises numerous questions. Why did Uthman destroy the original copies of the Qur'an? Weren't they genuine revelations? If so, how could he destroy? How accurate were the written messages or the memories of those who first heard the prophet? Were the diverse sources from which the Qur'an was compiled equally reliable? If so, why destroy them? Did Muhammad ever claim inspiration—even when he was not inspired?

A terrifying visitation

Khadija, Muhammad's wife, said that at times Muhammad would roar like a camel and roll on the floor. Whatever the revelation was that he received, it was apparently terrifying him. According to Ergun Caner, "As Buhkari's Hadith begins, it says that Muhammad really struggled with the issue of where this revelation comes from. Once Khadija tells him, 'No, no, no. These aren't demonic. These are from a God called Allah.'"[22]

Sources of corruption

We have already seen that the revelations were tampered with. In this regard, respected Muslim authority Guillaume further comments that

the Quran as we have it now is a record of what Muhammad said while in the [seizure] state or states just mentioned. It is beyond doubt that his hearers recognized the symptoms of revelation…[However,] one of the secretaries he employed boasted that he had induced the prophet to alter the wording of the revelations.[21]

Muslims may claim that the Arabic Qur'an is the same today as when it was first given to Muhammad, but this is simply not true. In *The Islam Debate*, Josh McDowell comments,

> The Qur'an's transmission is not free from errors and variant readings in significant points. There is concrete evidence in the best works of Islamic tradition (for example, *Sahih of Muslim*, the *Sahih of Bukhari*, the *Mishkat-ul-Masabih*), that from the start the Qur'an had numerous variant and conflicting readings. That these are no longer found in the Qur'an is only because they have been discreetly removed—not by direction of God, but by human discretion. There is similar evidence that, to this day, verses and, indeed, whole passages are still missing from the Qur'an.[23]

Dr. Anis Shorrosh, an Arab Christian, concludes his own study of the Qur'an thus:

> It is not the Bible which is contradictory and confusing. No, it is definitely the Quran. If Muslims insist that the Bible is corrupt, I will have to declare that the evidence, much of which I have presented in this book, vindicates the Bible and condemns the Quran. No reasonable person presented with the evidence can believe otherwise.[24]

In conclusion, Muslims have never proven that the Bible has been corrupted. But sufficient evidence exists to show the Qur'an was.

17

Can the Qur'an be objectively interpreted?

Dr. J. Christy Wilson comments about the problems of correctly interpreting the Qur'an, when some of its verses are said to either supersede other verses or cancel them out:

> It is most difficult for one who is not a Muslim to understand the theory that the Koran was inscribed from all eternity on a tablet in heaven, because some verses supersede and cancel others…Even to Muslims much of the text is unintelligible except through a commentary…It is kept with the utmost reverence, only touched after ceremonial ablutions, and read or recited by many millions of Muslims who do not understand the meaning of its Arabic verses.[25]

The Qur'an was originally written in a script that made no indication of vowels or diacritical points. Therefore, "*Variant readings* are recognized by Muslims *as of equal authority*" and "it ought to be borne in mind that the Koran contains many statements which, if not recognized as altogether obscure, lend themselves to more than one interpretation."[26]

In Sura 2:100 the Qur'an itself teaches, "And for whatever verse We abrogate or cast into oblivion, We bring a better or the like of it; knowest thou not that God is powerful over everything?"[27] This verse may serve the Muslim as a rationale for contradictions between the Qur'an and the Bible or the Qur'an and itself, but what does it say about Allah and his ability to communicate his Word clearly and effectively? Nowhere in the Qur'an does Allah identify those verses he has repealed or destroyed. How then does the Muslim know which verses are legitimate—and which are not?

How can anyone know the meaning?

Further, the Qur'an teaches that its ambiguous parts *cannot* be interpreted:

> It is He who sent down upon thee the Book, wherein are verses clear that are the Essence of the Book, and others ambiguous. As for those in whose hearts is swerving, they follow the ambiguous part, desiring dissension, and desiring its interpretation; and none knows its interpretation, save only God. And those firmly rooted in knowledge say, "We believe in it; all is from our Lord"; yet none remembers, but men possessed of minds.[28]

Here we are told the clear verses are the *essence* of the Qur'an. If so, we could assume Muslims would rarely disagree as to the interpretation of the clear parts. But is this what we find historically or today? Unfortunately, no. Have Muslims ever identified which are the "clear" parts and which are the "ambiguous" parts? No.

So, if much of the Qur'an is to varying degrees unclear, on what objective basis can one determine its meaning? And if the material is unessential, why record or reveal it in the first place? Also, how does an individual Muslim know all that is involved in having a "swerving" heart or how this relates to knowing the location of the ambiguous parts? The Qur'an also claims, "Those who have been given the Book know it is the truth from their Lord."[29] But in light of what we have discussed so far, upon what *objective* basis can a Muslim know this? The evidence contradicts such a claim.

As we saw, the Qur'an teaches that Allah occasionally changes his mind concerning the validity of his word. Here and there one verse is exchanged for another. But when critics in Muhammad's own day pointed this out and charged him with tampering, they themselves were charged with ignorance:

> And when We exchange a verse in the place of another verse—and God knows very well what He is sending down—they say, "Thou art a mere forger!" Nay, but the most of them have no knowledge.[30]

Another translation reads,

> When We change one verse for another (Allah knows best what He reveals), they say: "You are an impostor." Indeed, most of them are ignorant men.[31]

Allah may know best what he reveals, but again, how are mere humans expected to sort out the meaning? How does a Muslim authoritatively decide which verse is "exchanged" or now preferred by Allah? Further, why would Allah exchange one verse for another one to begin with? Why wouldn't he just speak clearly the first time?

These are more than mere academic issues. Muslims trust in the Qur'an for their eternal salvation. But if Muslims are uncertain of what God says—and of his intention—how can they know God's will? How can they ever hope to find salvation? By contrast, both Christians and Muslims can know exactly what Jesus Christ taught because his words have never been changed or corrupted. In our final question we will see why.

The Accuracy of the
New Testament Text

18

Can it be proved that the New Testament text is historically reliable and accurate?

Christians and skeptical non-Christians, including Muslims and members of religious groups like Mormonism, have different views concerning the credibility of the Gospels and the rest of the New Testament.

Dr. Ergun Caner made the following observations in one of our television programs:

> Anyone can teach in their church and explain what Islam basically is like this: It's medieval Mormonism. What Joseph Smith did in the nineteenth century, Muhammad did in the seventh and eighth century.
>
> Think of it. Number one, they both said that all the world was corrupt, that Christianity was corrupt, and there was no true religion on the planet when they both came. Joseph Smith said this, Muhammad said this.
>
> Both of them said they received a revelation from an angel—Moroni, Smith said, or the angel Jibrael, Muhammad said.
>
> Both said they received the revelation from tablets—golden tablets. Both sets are preserved—buried in Mormonism, in Paradise in the case of Islam.
>
> Both of them taught that Judaism had the truth but lost it; Christianity had the truth but lost it; and now they were here as the final word.

Both of them teach that Jesus was a prophet, but not the one and only God. Both of them teach that Jesus said that He would send a final prophet—Mormonism says Joseph Smith, Islam says Muhammad.

Both of them teach that salvation is all works.

Both of them have Jesus as a celestial brother—that is, in sort of a "one of us" position, but not as God in any sense.

Both of them teach that women, in eternity, will be sexual servants. In Islam a woman is a *houri*—she is one of the virgins, waiting on the martyrs. And in Mormonism she's eternally pregnant, a celestial bride.

And so, when you explain this, sometimes the light goes on in somebody's eyes and they say, "Oh!" because it's nothing new. The devil has no new lies. He just keeps rehashing the same things.[1]

But the main question we are examining now is, "Can Christianity prove that Islam is wrong in what it says about the Bible being corrupted?" For the Christian, nothing is more vital than the very words of Jesus himself, who promised, "Heaven and earth will pass away, but my words will never pass away" (Matthew 24:35). Jesus' promise is no small matter. If his words were *not* accurately recorded in the Gospels, how can anyone know what he really taught? The truth is, we *couldn't* know. Further, if the remainder of the New Testament cannot be established to be historically reliable, then little if anything can be known about what true Christianity really is, teaches, or means.

Examining the text and examining critical methods

Christians maintain that anyone who desires can

prove to their own satisfaction that, on the basis of accepted bibliographic, internal, external, and other criteria, the New Testament text can be established as reliable. Textually, we know we have over 99 percent accuracy in the transmission of the New Testament text, with the remaining 1 percent found in variant readings. Textual scholars tell us that no Christian doctrine or moral teaching rests upon a disputed variant reading, the vast majority of which are insignificant.[2] Thus there is simply no legitimate basis upon which to doubt the credibility and accuracy of the New Testament's human authors.

Further, the methods used by the critics Muslims so often rely on—rationalist, higher-critical methods that claim the New Testament is unreliable—have been judged by much *secular* scholarship as biased and unfounded. Their use in biblical analysis is therefore unjustified. Relative to the biblical text, even in a positive sense, the fruit these critical methods have borne is minuscule; negatively, they are responsible for a tremendous weight of destruction: confusion over biblical authority and the trustworthiness of the Bible and the logical consequences in people's lives. Fair-minded biblical critics would have to agree that higher criticism's 200-year failure to prove its case strengthens by default the conservative Christian view of biblical inspiration and reliability.

Considering the evidence

Those critics who continue to advance discredited theories about the New Testament should listen to the warnings of Chauncey Sanders, a scholar in history and literature. A literary critic, Sanders notes, should be certain he is careful to examine *all* the evidence, pro and con:

He must be as careful to collect evidence against his theory as for it. It may go against the grain to be very assiduous in searching for ammunition to destroy one's own case; but it must be remembered that the overlooking of a single detail may be fatal to one's whole argument. Moreover, it is the business of the scholar to seek the truth, and the satisfaction of having found it should be ample recompense for having to give up a cherished but untenable theory.[3]

Resolving the question

The fair-minded Muslim or skeptic can resolve the issue of New Testament reliability by recognizing that the following ten facts cannot logically be denied.*

Fact one. The existence of 5,700 Greek manuscripts and portions of the New Testament, another 10,000 copies in Latin Vulgate, and another 10,000 to 15,000 in other versions—along with the numerous papyri and early uncial manuscripts dating much closer to the original than for any other piece of ancient literature—coalesce to prove the New Testament has not been corrupted.

Fact two. The lack of proven fraud or error on the part of *any* New Testament author shows that the writers were trustworthy in what they wrote.

Fact three. Reliable Christian sources outside the New Testament also confirm its integrity. There are hundreds of thousands of quotations of the New Testament found in the writings of the Church Fathers. If every copy of the New Testament that has come down to us were lost, we could still reconstruct the entire New Testament (except for 11 verses) from the quotes of these early church writers. This is also material that can be

---

* We have discussed each of these points and provided documentation in our *Handbook of Biblical Evidences* (Harvest House, 2008) and *The Facts on Why You Can Believe the Bible* (Harvest House, 2004).

compared to the manuscript copies to see if any errors took place in transmission.

Fact four. The existence of a number of Jewish and secular accounts about Jesus confirms several basic New Testament teachings.

Fact five. Detailed archaeological data concerning the New Testament proves the authors wrote with care and accuracy.

Fact six. The many powerful first-century enemies of Jesus and the early church would have proven fraud or pointed out other problems if they could have, but they never did. The reason is, they had nothing to appeal to.

Fact seven. The presence of numerous credible living eyewitnesses to the events recorded, especially of Jesus' death and resurrection, offers powerful evidence as to the truth of what was recorded. All of the 27 books of the New Testament were written or approved by one of six unimpeachable sources: the apostles Matthew, Peter, Paul, John, James, or Jude (or seven, if the author of Hebrews was not the apostle Paul).

Fact eight. Positive appraisals have come from conservative and even some liberal authorities, which bear on the issue of the genuineness of traditional authorship and the early date of the New Testament books. This further confirms their integrity.

Fact nine. There are consistent scholarly, factual reversals of the negative conclusions of higher criticism, which undermine that method's foundations and credibility.

Fact ten. There is powerful legal and other testimony as to New Testament reliability.

These facts demonstrate the accuracy and reliability of the New Testament beyond reasonable doubt. As an example of the multiplicity and detail of New Testament evidences, let us examine the final point from the ten facts above.

Corroboration from legal testimony and former skeptics

We must acknowledge the historicity of the New Testament when we consider that many great minds of legal history have, on the grounds of strict legal reasoning and evidence alone, accepted the New Testament as reliable history. This is not to mention that, since the time of Christ, many skeptical intellects have converted to Christianity on the basis of the historical evidence—including Saul of Tarsus, Athenagoras, Augustine, George Lyttleton and Gilbert West, C.S. Lewis, Frank Morison, Sir William Ramsay, John Warwick Montgomery, and Lee Strobel.

Lawyers, of course, are expertly trained in the matter of evaluating evidence and are perhaps the most qualified in the task of weighing data critically. Is it coincidence that so many of them throughout history have concluded in favor of the truth of the Christian religion? Consider, for example:

- the "father of international law," Hugo Grotius, who wrote *The Truth of the Christian Religion* (1627);

- the greatest authority in English and American common-law evidence in the nineteenth century, Harvard Law School professor Simon Greenleaf, who wrote *Testimony of the Evangelists*, in which he powerfully demonstrated the reliability of the gospels;[4]

- Edmund H. Bennett (1824–1898), for over 20 years the dean of Boston University Law School, who penned *The Four Gospels from a Lawyer's Standpoint* (1899);[5]

- Irwin Linton, who in his time represented cases before the Supreme Court and wrote *A Lawyer Examines the Bible* (1943, 1977).

The irresistible force of the evidence

Attorney Irwin Linton's words are an example of the kind of conclusion legal minds have reached about the facts on the Bible:

> So invariable had been my observation that he who does not accept wholeheartedly the evangelical, conservative belief in Christ and the Scriptures has never read, has forgotten, or never been able to weigh—and certainly is utterly unable to refute—the irresistible force of the cumulative evidence upon which such faith rests, that there seems ample ground for the conclusion that such ignorance is an invariable element in such unbelief. And this is so even though the unbeliever be a preacher, who is supposed to know this subject if he know no other.[6]

Moreover, hundreds of contemporary lawyers—also on the grounds of strict legal evidence—accept the New Testament as historically accurate. And consider Jacques Ellul, the great French philosopher and author, or J.N.D. (Sir Norman) Anderson, one of the greatest authorities on Islamic law, also a Christian convinced of NT authority and reliability.

Beyond a reasonable doubt. Certainly such intellects are well-acquainted with legal reasoning and have just as certainly concluded that the evidence for the historic truthfulness of the Scriptures is beyond reasonable doubt. John W. Montgomery, apologist, theologian, and lawyer, in *The Law Above the Law,* takes into account 1) the "ancient documents" rule—that ancient documents constitute competent evidence if there is no evidence of tampering and they have been accurately transmitted; 2) the "parol evidence" rule—Scripture must interpret itself without foreign intervention; 3) the "hearsay" rule—the demand for primary-source evidence; and 4) the "cross examination" principle—the inability of the enemies of Christianity to disprove, in spite of the motive and opportunity to do so, its central claim: that Christ was resurrected bodily from the dead. All these, concludes Montgomery, coalesce directly or indirectly to support the preponderance of evidence for Christianity—while the burden of proof proper (the legal burden) for disproving it rests with the critic, who, in 2,000 years, has yet to prove his case.[7]

What can we conclude? To reject the New Testament accounts as true history is, by definition, to reject the canons of legitimate historical study. To reject the Gospels or the New Testament is to reject primary historical documentation in general. If this cannot be done, the New Testament must be retained as careful historical reporting. It has proven itself reliable in the crucible of history and all variety of criticism. It is the New Testament *critic* who has been unable to prove his case. The implications are immense. Legal scholar J.N.D. Anderson observes in *Christianity: The Witness of History:*

> It seems to me inescapable that anyone who chanced to read the pages of the New Testament for the first time would come away with one overwhelming

impression—that here is a faith firmly rooted in certain allegedly historical events, a faith which would be false and misleading if those events had not actually taken place, but which, if they did take place, is unique in its relevance and exclusive in its demands on our allegiance. For these events did not merely set a "process in motion and then themselves sink back into the past. The unique historical origin of Christianity is ascribed permanent, authoritative, absolute significance; what happened once is said to have happened once for all and therefore to have continuous efficacy."[8]

Muslim claims are simply not credible

In essence, the Muslim claim that the New Testament has been textually corrupted is untrue and demonstrably false. That claim can never be substantiated, due to the vast amount of textual and other evidence at hand. Simply put, facts are facts.

What about the Muslim claim that Christians have so severely misinterpreted their own Scriptures that they teach a false view of God, Jesus, salvation, or other issues? We must remember that we have had almost 2,000 years of universally accepted Christian doctrine—doctrine that even skeptics of Christianity freely acknowledge the Bible teaches. This is why anyone who wishes can determine the basic doctrine of the New Testament just by studying it.

In conclusion, Muslim claims relative to the New Testament are simply not credible. We can only trust that, as some have done in every generation since Islam was founded, Muslims today will impartially investigate the evidence for New Testament authenticity and respond according to that evidence.

19

What can Muslims do who desire to *know* that they have eternal life?

If you are a Muslim who is willing to accept the evidence and who desires to *know* you have eternal life (the single most precious item available in this life), what can you do? Jesus promises all people who believe on him—not just that he is a prophet, but that he is God in human form—that they can know they *now* possess eternal life:

- "This is eternal life, that they may *know* You, the only true God, and Jesus Christ whom You have sent" (John 17:3 NASB).

- "Truly, truly, I say to you, he who believes *has eternal life*" (John 6:47 NASB).

- "I tell you the truth, whoever hears my word and believes him who sent me *has eternal life* and will not be condemned; he has *crossed over* from death to life" (John 5:24).

- "My sheep listen to my voice; I know them, and they follow me. *I give them eternal life*, and they shall *never perish*; no one can snatch them out of my hand" (John 10:27-28).

If you have longed for a personal relationship with God, a relationship in which you know that God loves you, and have been unable to find this in Islam, then the one true God offers you this opportunity. God tells us that "all have sinned and fall short of the glory of God" (Romans 3:23). God has promised us full forgiveness of sins (Hebrews 10:14) if we turn from our sin and turn to Christ, believing on him for salvation: "The wages of sin is death, but the gift of God is eternal life in Christ Jesus our Lord" (Romans 6:23). Jesus said,

> God so loved the world that he gave his one and only Son, that whoever believes in him shall not perish but have eternal life. For God did not send his Son into the world to condemn the world, but to save the world through him. Whoever believes in him is not condemned, but whoever does not believe stands condemned already because he has not believed in the name of God's one and only Son (John 3:16-18).

And the apostle John wrote,

> We accept man's testimony, but God's testimony is greater because it is the testimony of God, which he has given about his Son. Anyone who believes in the Son of God has this testimony in his heart. Anyone who does not believe God has made him out to be a liar, because he has not believed the testimony God has given about his Son. And this is the testimony: God has given us eternal life, and this life is in his Son. He who has the Son has life; he who does not have the Son of God does not have life. I write these things to you who believe in the name of the Son of God so that you may know that you have eternal life (1 John 5:9-13).

What to do

If you sincerely desire to know God personally, to know that all your sins are forgiven—and want to be certain that a place in heaven *is* reserved for you (1 Peter 1:4-5)—you can gain these things by praying the following prayer to receive Jesus Christ as your personal Lord and Savior:

Dear God,

I acknowledge my sinfulness before you. I confess I have been trying to earn my own salvation by following the teachings of the Qur'an. But I now realize that Allah is not the true God. I recognize my need for forgiveness and now understand that Christ died for my sins on the cross so I wouldn't have to be punished. I now receive him as my personal Savior and Lord. Come into my life, live in me, and give me courage and strength to face the opposition I may encounter. Help me to lead others to you as well. In Jesus' name I pray. Amen.

If you have prayed this prayer, please write us at *The John Ankerberg Show* or e-mail us at **staff@johnankerberg.org** so we can send you some helpful materials about growing in the Christian life. We also recommend that you begin to read the New Testament to know more about the true Jesus Christ. In addition, attend a church that honors Christ as Lord and the Bible as God's Word. Talk to God daily in prayer. For additional spiritual growth resources, please visit our Web site at **johnankerberg.org.**

RECOMMENDED RESOURCES

Books:

Abdul-Haqq, Abdiyah Akbar. *Sharing Your Faith with a Muslim*. Minneapolis: Bethany, 1980.

Anderson, J.N.D. *Christianity and Comparative Religion*. Downer's Grove, IL: InterVarsity, 1970 ed.

Bar, Samuel. *Warrant for Terror: The Fatwas of Radical Islam*.

Boston, Andrew. *The Legacy of Jihad*.

Cook, David. *Understanding Jihad*. Berkeley, CA: University of California Press, 2005.

Davis, Gregory. *Islam: A Religion of Peace?*

Gilchrist, John, and Josh McDowell. *The Islam Debate*. San Bernardino, CA: Here's Life Publishers, 1983.

Ibrahim, Raymond. *The al-Qaeda Reader*.

Marsh, C.R. *Share Your Faith with a Muslim*. Chicago: Moody, 1976.

Morey, Robert A. *Islamic Invasion*. Eugene, OR: Harvest House, 1992.

North Africa Mission. *Reaching Muslims Today: A Short Handbook*. Upper Darby, PA: North Africa Mission, 1982.

Shoebat, Walad. *Why We Want to Kill You*. Newton, PA: Top Executive Media, 2007

Additional important materials are available through the Web sites of the following organizations:

AlwaysBeReady.com. The Web site of speaker and author Charlie Campbell, which includes several Muslim articles and media resources.

ApologeticsIndex.org. A huge directory of free apologetics resources featuring a quality overview of Islam with documented links.

AWM.Gospelcom.net. Arab World Ministries Web site. The organization describes itself as "a multinational body of believers seeking to reach Arabs worldwide."

BeThinking.org. Apologetics resources for free, with several specific to Islam, from a European Evangelical perspective.

CARM.org. The Christian Apologetics Resource Ministry (CARM) with a selection of short-answer articles on aspects of Islam as it relates to Christianity.

CIU.edu/MuslimStudies. The Web site of the Zwemer Center for Muslim Studies, part of Columbia International University.

DanielPipes.org. Commentary from Daniel Pipes on current issues dealing with Islam.

EmirCaner.com. A former Muslim turned Christian professor who frequently writes and speaks on issues of Islam and Christianity.

ErgunCaner.com. A former Muslim who is now a Christian and president of Liberty Baptist Theological Seminary.

F-F-M.org.uk. Fellowship of Faith for the Muslims, an organization based in the United Kingdom.

FutureOfMuslimWorld.com. The Web site of the Center on Islam, Democracy, and the Future of the Muslim World at the Hudson Institute.

HorizonsInternational.org. The Web site of Horizons International

ImpactApologetics.com. An online store representing a wide selection of apologetics-specific materials, including several audio downloads.

JihadWatch.org. Jihad Watch provides a variety of articles and commentary on current developments in worldwide Islam.

LeaderU.edu. This Campus Crusade for Christ resource offers an extensive array of academic articles on world religions, including many on Islam.

LeeStrobel.com. This Web site offers short video clips of leading scholars debating issues of Islam from a Christian perspective.

MEForum.org. The Middle East Forum Web site. The organization calls itself a "think tank" that "seeks to define and promote American interests in the Middle East."

MissionBooks.org/WilliamCareyLibrary. The William Carey Library at the U.S. Center for World Missions offers resources for "global trends, fruitful practices, and emerging issues among Muslims."

SecularIslam.org. The Secular Islam Summit seeks to foster "a new Enlightenment, or a secularization and liberalization of Islamic thought and practice." It brings together "thinkers and activists in an ongoing cross-cultural forum and clearinghouse."

TheirOwnWords.com. This organization asks the question, "Are we in danger from radical jihadists?" and "features constantly-updated examples of statements by religious extremists concerning the United States, Western Civilization, Israel and Christianity."

NOTES

Note to reader: Sura references are taken either from the Arberry, Rodwell, Dawood, or Ali translations. Translators differ somewhat in their numbering of verses; verses may be off by two or three, or paragraphs may be numbered rather than verses. Some translations do not number either verses or paragraphs. Chapters are also numbered differently in English and Arabic.

Encouraging Communication and Critique

1. J.N.D. (Sir Norman) Anderson, ed., *The World's Religions* (Downer's Grove, IL: InterVarsity, 1976, rev.), p. 91.

2. J. Christy Wilson, *Introducing Islam* (New York: Friendship Press, 1965, rev. ed.), p. 30.

3. A.J. Arberry, *The Koran Interpreted* (New York: MacMillan, 1976), cover statement.

4. Robert A. Morey, *Islamic Invasion* (Eugene, OR: Harvest House, 1992), p. 175.

5. C. George Fry and James R. King, *Islam: A Survey of the Muslim Faith* (Grand Rapids: Baker, 1981), p. 38.

6. Stephen Neill, *Christian Faith and Other Faiths* (Downer's Grove, IL: InterVarsity, 1984), p. 63.

Section One: The Religion of Islam—Introduction

1. Walter R. Martin, "The Black Muslim Cult," *The Kingdom of the Cults* (Minneapolis: Bethany, 1970 ed.), pp. 259-75.

2. Based on a 2001 survey: see www.adherents.com/largecom/com_islam_usa.html. For more recent figures, consult www.danielpipes.org and www.adherents.com.

3. Robert Morey, *Islamic Invasion* (Eugene, OR: Harvest House, 1992), pp. 21-23; other materials from the organizations cited in "Recommended Resources." See also John Ankerberg and John Weldon, *One World: Bible Prophecy and the New World Order* (Chicago: Moody Press, 1991), pp. 110-20.

4. Morey, pp. 21-23.

5. Jonathan Dowd-Gailey, "Islamism's Campus Club," *Middle East Quarterly*, June 2, 2004, accessed at www.frontpagemag.com/Articles/Read.aspx?GUID= percent7BE530BEFF-AE61-4DD6-BE0E-D796BA57FC2Epercent7D; "Islamic Architecture, Art, and Urbanism," MIT University Library, October, 13, 2004, accessed at http://libraries.mit.edu/guides/subjects/islamicarchitecture/visual/ usamosques.html. Also see various Web sites such as wikipedia.org and adherents .com.

6. A.M. Holt, ed., *The Cambridge History of Islam*, vol. 2 (London: Cambridge University Press, 1970), cited in Josh McDowell and John Gilchrist, *The Islam Debate* (San Bernardino, CA: Here's Life Publishers, 1983), p. 16.

7. J.N.D. (Sir Norman) Anderson, ed., *The World's Religions* (Grand Rapids: Eerdmans, 1966), pp. 54;60; see also Morey, pp. 69-88,93-99.

8. Robert Payne, *The Holy Sword* (New York: Collier, 1962), cited in McDowell and Gilchrist, p. 15.

9. John Elder, *The Biblical Approach to the Muslim* (Fort Washington, PA: World-wide Evangelization Crusade, 1978), pp. 30-31; McDowell and Gilchrist, p. 19 passim.

10. Emir Caner, "What Islam Teaches about Jesus' Return, Armageddon, Jerusalem, and the Jews," *The John Ankerberg Show*, 2006. The transcript has been slightly edited for clarity.

Section Two: The Theology of Islam—Is It Compatible with Christian Belief?

1. A.J. Arberry, *The Koran Interpreted* (New York: MacMillan, 1976), p. 15,65.

2. Arberry, p. 140.

3. Arberry, pp. 139-40. See our *Knowing the Truth About the Trinity* (Eugene, OR: Harvest House, 1997). Also see E. Calvin Bisner, *God in Three Persons* (Wheaton, IL: Tyndale, 1984) and Edward Bickersteth, *The Trinity* (Grand Rapids, MI: Kregel, rpt.).

4. For example, Arberry, pp. 81,90,142,178,204.

5. Cited in a book review in *Reach Out*, vol. 6, nos. 3 and 4, 1993, p. 15.

6. Georges Houssney, "What Is Allah Like?" *Reach Out*, vol. 6, nos. 3 and 4, 1993, pp. 12-13.

7. This involves the Qur'an as interpreted by Muslim clerics (see question 17); to submit to the "will of Allah," is to submit to the religious leaders' interpretations of the Qur'an, which involve everything relating to life, including Islamic law, politics, cultural customs, family, and so on. To submit to Allah is to submit to the Islamic powers that be. The concept of separation of church and state is never found in Muslim nations.

8. Houssney.

9. For example, Sura 3:45.

10. Arberry, p. 64.

11. Biblically, Christ's designation as God's Son is a declaration of his deity (John 5:18; 19:7), but Muslims have other objections to Christ being God's Son.

12. N.J. Dawood, *The Koran* (Baltimore: Penguin Books, 1972), pp. 34,233,315,316, 130.

13. J.N.D. (Sir Norman) Anderson, *Christianity and Comparative Religion* (Downer's Grove, IL: InterVarsity, 1970 ed.), p. 47.

14. A. Yusuf Ali, *The Holy Qur'an* (Washington, D.C.: The Islamic Center, 1978), p. 266.

15. *Tawhid* is the doctrine of the singularity of Allah; *shirk* is its opposite, the greatest of all sins. It refers to assigning partners or companions to Allah.

16. Arberry, p. 125; Dawood, p. 149.

17. Arberry, p. 147.

18. Badru D. Kateregga and David W. Shenk, *Islam and Christianity: A Muslim and a Christian in Dialogue* (Grand Rapids: Eerdmans, 1980), p. 37, emphasis added.

19. Ergun and Emir Caner, from an interview on *The John Ankerberg Show*. The transcript has been slightly edited for clarity.

20. Arberry, pp. 75,85,48.

21. Arberry, respectively, pp. 93,220,344; for the last, compare pp. 102,105.

22. Sura 23:104-105 in the George Sale translation (1734), as cited by Phillip H. Lochhaas, *How to Respond to Islam* (St. Louis: Concordia, 1981), p. 24.

23. Dawood, p. 241.

24. Abdiyah Akbar Abdul-Haqq, *Sharing Your Faith with a Muslim* (Minneapolis: Bethany, 1980), p. 164.

25. William Miller, *A Christian's Response to Islam* (Nutley, NJ: Presbyterian and Reformed, 1977), pp. 82-83.

26. Arberry, p. 58.

27. Ibid., p. 143.

28. Dawood, p. 372.

29. In Josh McDowell and John Gilchrist, *The Islam Debate* (San Bernardino, CA: Here's Life Publishers, 1983), p. 172.

30. John Elder, *The Biblical Approach to the Muslim* (Fort Washington, PA: World-wide Evangelization Crusade, 1978), pp. 94-96. Dr. Elder's scholarly works include 11 books in Farsi (Persian) and 2 in English.

31. J. Christy Wilson, *Introducing Islam* (New York: Friendship Press, 1965, rev. ed.), p. 20.

32. Elder, p. 59.

33. J.M. Rodwell, *The Koran* (New York: Dutton, 1977), p. 78; Arberry, p. 274.

34. Abdul-Haqq, p. 159.

35. Wilson, p. 24; Arberry, p. 111.

36. Dawood, p. 256, emphasis added.

37. Arberry, p. 93; compare p. 98.

38. Dawood, pp. 212-22.

39. Dawood, pp. 367-68.

40. Arberry, pp. 198-99.

41. Arberry, pp. 139-40.

42. Rodwell, p. 471.

43. Arberry, p. 214.

44. Rodwell, p. 417.

Section Three: The Bible of Islam—Is the Qur'an the Word of God?

1. Musa Qutub and M. Vazir Ali, "The Glorious Quran—The Unique Divine Document for Mankind," in *The Invitation*, Nov. 1987, vol. 4, no. 4, Des Plaines, IL: p. 1.

2. A.J. Arberry, *The Koran Interpreted* (New York: MacMillan, 1976), p. 135.

3. Arberry, p. 229.

4. *Encyclopedia Britannica*, 1958 ed.

5. Robert Morey, *Islamic Invasion* (Eugene, OR: Harvest House Publishers, 1992), pp. 137-58.

6. J.M. Rodwell, *The Koran* (New York: Dutton, 1977), p. 3.

7. N.J. Dawood, *The Koran* (Baltimore: Penguin Books, 1972), p. 253; Rodwell, p. 499.

8. Arberry, p. 83.

9. Dawood, p. 254.

10. Anis A. Shorrosh, *Islam Revealed: A Christian Arab's View of Islam* (Nashville: Nelson, 1998), pp. 201-19,140.

11. Dawood, pp. 291-92; 101:194; Rodwell, pp. 473-74n; Arberry, pp. 63,83,138, 158,185 (compare 258), 187-88,190,314,331,348; see also Gleason L. Archer, *A Survey of Old Testament Introduction*, rev. ed. (Chicago: Moody Press, 1985), "Appendix on Errors in Koran," pp. 506-08.

12. Don Wismer, *The Islamic Jesus: An Annotated Bibliography of Sources in English and French* (New York: Garland Publishing, 1977); compare Arberry, pp. 242-60; Dawood, pp. 324-32,339,348,285,175-81,319, etc.; compare Rodwell, p. 105.

13. Arberry, pp. 135,229; see question 13.

14. Dawood, p. 365.

15. Dawood, pp. 134,294.

16. For more such examples, see Morey.

Section Four: Islam—A General Critique

1. John Warwick Montgomery, "How Muslims Do Apologetics," in *Faith Founded on Fact: Essays and Evidential Apologetics* (Nashville, TN: Nelson, 1978), p. 93.

2. For example, Khalid Jan, in his attack on biblical authority in *A Human Bible* (draft), cites such biased sources as the Jesus Seminar's *The Five Gospels* and G.A. Wells's *Who Was Jesus?*—while taking other sources out of context. Compare various Muslim Internet sites.

3. For an illustration, see John Weldon, "Letters to the Editor," in the *Athens [GA] Banner-Herald*, Oct. 2, 1989.

4. Available from the California Institute of Apologetics. Also see Morey's "Muslims and Their Logical Fallacies," *The Truth Seeker*, Jan. 1997, as well as other debates and materials, including those in the "Recommended Resources." The interested reader should also secure literature from American Islamic societies—for example, The Islamic Center, Washington, DC, as it relates to their treatment of Christianity.

5. A.J. Arberry, *The Koran Interpreted* (New York: MacMillan, 1976), p. 85, emphasis added.

6. Arberry, p. 35; N.J. Dawood, *The Koran* (Baltimore: Penguin Books, 1972) p. 384.

7. Arberry, pp. 120-21.

8. Arberry, p. 122.

9. Abdiyah Akbar Abdul-Haqq, *Sharing Your Faith with a Muslim* (Minneapolis: Bethany, 1980), pp. 22-31,38-46,50-53,67-73; Arberry, pp. 185,199,120-22.

10. Arberry, p. 130.

11. Stephen Neill, *Christian Faith and Other Faiths*, 2nd ed. (New York: Oxford University Press, 1970), p. 64.

12. See Robert Morey, *Islamic Invasion* (Eugene, OR: Harvest House, 1992), pp. 129-32,136; and our note 4 above.

13. Norman Geisler and William Nix, *A General Introduction to the Bible* (Chicago: Moody Press, 1971); compare F.F. Bruce, *The New Testament Documents: Are They Reliable?* (Downer's Grove, IL: InterVarsity, 1981); and John Warwick

Montgomery, *History and Christianity* (San Bernardino, CA: Campus Crusade for Christ, 1982).

14. Geisler and Nix, p. 375; compare pp. 238,267,365-66.

15. Morey, pp. 117-20.

16. Morey, pp. 120-26.

17. J.M. Rodwell, *The Koran* (New York: Dutton, 1977), p. 1; Alfred Guillaume, *Islam* (New York: Penguin Books, 1977), p. 57.

18. Miller, p. 52, emphasis added; Elder, p. 27.

19. Guillaume, p. 57, emphasis added.

20. Robert E. Hume, *The World's Living Religions*, rev. ed. (New York: Charles Scribner's Sons, 1959), p. 229.

21. Guillaume, p. 56.

22. Ergun Caner, in "Former Muslims Testify," *The John Ankerberg Show*, 2003. The transcript has been slightly edited for clarity.

23. McDowell and Gilchrist, pp. 50-51.

24. Anis A. Shorrosh, *Islam Revealed: A Christian Arab's View of Islam* (Nashville: Nelson, 1998), pp. 197-98.

25. J. Christy Wilson, *Introducing Islam* (New York: Friendship Press, 1965, rev. ed.), pp. 29-30.

26. Dawood, pp. 10-11, emphasis added. The script style is known as *Kufic*.

27. Arberry, p. 41.

28. Arberry, p. 73.

29. Arberry, p. 46.

30. Arberry, p. 298.

31. Dawood, p. 304.

Section Five: The Accuracy of the New Testament Text

1. Ergun Caner, in "Where Is Islam Taking the World?" *The John Ankerberg Show*, 2006. The transcript has been slightly edited for clarity.

2. See our program, "The Battle to Discredit the Bible," *The John Ankerberg Show*, 2007.

3. Chauncey Sanders, *An Introduction to Research in English Literary History* (New York: MacMillan, 1952), p. 160. Sanders was an associate professor of military history, Air University, Maxwell Air Force Base, Montgomery, AL. His comments were specifically in reference to the authenticity or authorship of a given text.

4. Reprinted in John Warwick Montgomery, *The Law Above the Law* (Minneapolis: Bethany, 1975), appendix, pp. 91-140.

5. Reprinted in *The Simon Greenleaf Law Review*, vol. 1 (Orange, CA: The Faculty of the Simon Greenleaf School of Law, 1981–82), pp. 15,74.

6. Irwin Linton, *A Lawyer Examines the Bible* (San Diego: Creation Life Publishers, 1977), p. 45.

7. John Warwick Montgomery, "Legal Reasoning and Christian Apologetics," in *The Law Above the Law* (Minneapolis: Bethany, 1975).

8. J.N.D. (Sir Norman) Anderson, *Christianity: The Witness of History* (Downer's Grove, IL: InterVarsity, 1970), pp. 13-14.

ABOUT THE ANKERBERG
THEOLOGICAL RESEARCH INSTITUTE

Asking tough questions...Offering real answers

Mission Statement

The Ankerberg Theological Research Institute (ATRI) is a Christian media organization designed to investigate and answer today's critical questions concerning issues of spirituality, popular culture, and comparative religions.

> *"But in your hearts set apart Christ as Lord. Always be prepared to give an answer to everyone who asks you to give the reason for the hope that you have. But do this with gentleness and respect, keeping a clear conscience, so that those who speak maliciously against your good behavior in Christ may be ashamed of their slander."*
>
> —1 PETER 3:15-16

ATRI utilizes five strategies to accomplish this mission:

- *The John Ankerberg Show.* Our weekly half-hour TV program reaches over 147 million people in the U.S., in addition to millions more worldwide via satellite. The award-winning *John Ankerberg Show* is considered the longest-running and most-established television program available today providing answers to issues of importance to Christians (also called apologetics). Its documentary specials have been featured as nationwide television specials.

- *ATRI Radio.* ATRI reaches thousands of people through its one-hour weekend program and new one-minute daily radio commentary that is being offered on over 130 stations nationwide.

- *JohnAnkerberg.org.* ATRI's Web site reaches nearly 3 million unique visitors per year from 184 countries, providing a truly global impact. ATRI continues to utilize today's newest media formats as well, including online audio and video downloads, podcasts, blogs, and mobile technologies.

- *ATRI Resources.* In addition to over 84 combined published books and 2.5 million books sold by ATRI authors in several languages, its resources include over 2,500 online articles that have been utilized as research by some of today's best-known media and academic organizations, both Christian and mainstream. In addition, ATRI offers transcripts of its TV interviews, which include thousands of hours of material from the past 28 years with top religious scholars.

- *ATRI Events.* Past speaking engagements have included Promise Keeper events, Focus on the Family seminars, and the National Apologetics Conference. Founder Dr. John Ankerberg has personally spoken to over one million people during his speaking and seminars in dozens of countries spanning five continents.

Due to ATRI's advanced research and long-standing work, founder and president Dr. John Ankerberg is regularly quoted in both Christian and mainstream media, including NBC, ABC, Daystar, and INSP, and has even testified before the U.S. Congressional Subcommittee on Financial Accountability for Christian Nonprofit Organizations. A board member for many Christian media organizations, Dr. Ankerberg also serves on the board of directors for the National Religious Broadcasters Association (NRB).

THE FACTS ON SERIES
John Ankerberg and John Weldon, with Dillon Burroughs

To read a sample chapter of these or other Harvest House books, go to www.harvesthousepublishers.com